THIS IS THE

LARA PAWSON

This Is the Place to Be

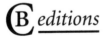

First published in the UK in 2016
by CB editions
146 Percy Road London W12 9QL
www.cbeditions.com

The right of Lara Pawson to be identified as author
of this work has been asserted in accordance with
the Copyright, Designs and Patents Act, 1988

Printed in England by T. J. International Ltd, Padstow

ISBN 978–1–909585–21–8

For you, J, of course

Freaks are called freaks and are treated as they are treated – in the main, abominably – because they are human beings who cause to echo, deep within us, our most profound terrors and desires.

Most of us, however, do not appear to be freaks – though we are rarely what we appear to be. We are, for the most part, visibly male or female, our social roles defined by our sexual equipment.

But we are all androgynous, not only because we are all born of a woman impregnated by the seed of a man but because each of us, helplessly and forever, contains the other – male in female, female in male, white in black and black in white. We are a part of each other. Many of my countrymen appear to find this fact exceedingly inconvenient and even unfair, and so, very often, do I. But none of us can do anything about it.

– James Baldwin, 'Freaks and the American Ideal of Manhood' (*Playboy*, January 1985)

When I was about seven the owner of a watch and clock shop mistook me for a boy. Twenty-four years later, a Nigerian man, following my radio reports from Angola, mistook me for a Nigerian. Omolara was what he called me.

When I had short hair I was regularly mistaken for Jamie Lee Curtis. In London, I've been followed by people with cameras. While visiting the Alhambra last year, a North American man pretended to take photographs of the Patio de los Leones but he was actually snapping me. I heard him whisper to his wife and I felt her eyes run over me. Once, when I was on a blind date, the owner of a restaurant in Soho invited me to sign the actress's account.

I've also been marched out of Primark for entering the women's changing room. One afternoon in Islington a group of men with shaved heads ran up the street shouting, Fucking trannie! One of them had a baseball bat. I remember looking around for the transvestite. Then I realised she was me.

Not long afterwards, I took the decision to grow my hair, a weakness that still shames me.

Today, some people call me Crofty. But there's an elderly man on my street – he's rebuilding a Morris Mini-Minor from scratch – well, he calls me Tomb Raider.

I have owned three tortoises. One of them could walk a mile in a weekend. His name was Maud. I also had a mouse called Charlotte, renamed Charlie when we noticed her testicles. Shortly after that, my brother's mouse produced lots of babies. They were so small and slender they could slip between the bars of the cage. For weeks, my mum kept finding squashed white mice beneath the fridge.

When I was living in Luanda I owned a Siamese cat. Fanny had been abandoned by her owners so I referred to her as an IDC – an internally displaced cat – as opposed to an IDP – an internally displaced person, which is United Nations-speak for people who are refugees inside their own country.

One day, Fanny gave birth to two kittens on my laptop. I was supposed to be filing a report to the BBC, but because of Fanny's labour I ended up filing the story an hour late. I wish I could remember what my news report was about that day. I wish I could remember how important it was.

During dinner with a crowd of aid workers, a British diplomat offered to adopt Fanny's kittens. He called one of them Madiba after Nelson Mandela. Among Europeans living in southern Africa, Madiba is – or certainly was – a popular pet's name. I met a foreign correspondent who had a pair of dogs: one called Madiba, the other called Graça after Graça Machel, Mandela's third wife. Or widow, as she is now.

I currently own two cats. They're called Lena and Salomão after the couple who looked after me in Luanda. I miss the real Lena and Salomão a lot. Sometimes I think the cats have become a bit like the people, but I don't trust that thought.

Memories creep up on me when I'm out walking. There's a lump of marble at the bottom of Coppermill Lane. There used to be a metal sculpture on top of it, made by local schoolchildren. But the sculpture was stolen, so the marble stands empty, a resting place on which to sit and stare. It looks like the trunk of a tree. Sawn-off and naked. I don't always notice it, but when I do I remember the soldier from M'banza Kongo.

We heard a gunshot. We ran with the crowds. There he was, on the stump of a tree. Sitting and staring. A rifle at his feet. His brains blown out through the back of his head.

To reach the marshes, I have to go down Coppermill batting away twists of insects which look like funnels of smoke spiralling skywards. To the north, reservoir number five is surrounded by a concrete palisade. Birders come here, pointing their binoculars towards the pair of islands in the centre of the water, to what is said to be one of the largest heron breeding sites in the UK. Grey herons, greylag geese, great-crested grebes, wagtails, wheatears, waders, the odd fisherman, the occasional fox.

I like the cormorants most. Large and conspicuous waterbirds, say the experts. I'd add the word haunting.

Sometimes, when I look through the gaps in the fence I can see the Cabinda swamps, the silhouettes of broken trees stretching north towards Congo. Another military checkpoint. A peak in anxiety because of my presence. My government minder hiding my notebook and recording equipment inside his jacket. I hear him mutter something about safety, then a reassurance: It's all right, don't look worried, they won't check me. He looks terrified.

I'd been in Angola just a few months and was already questioning what I was doing. How to report the nine-year-old boy who'd lost his legs after standing on a landmine? His parents dead, his siblings vanished, no aunties or uncles. The nurse said she was worried. He hadn't uttered a word since he was found by farmers a week earlier. I can still see the grey blanket on his hospital bed, the solemn quality of his face, the red water container beside his bed.

Two doctors from Vietnam were working around the clock, tidying up blasted bone, sewing up stumps and flesh and, No, Lara, they don't want to be interviewed.

I remember, back then, thinking about the first time I saw my parents cry. My mum was sitting at the wheel of the car outside our house in south-west London. My brother, my sister and I sat in the back, not knowing what to do. Perhaps my sister tried to comfort her. A quarter of a century later, my mum cried again, a few months after I'd written a letter about abortion to a national newspaper. I was in my twenties and was angry about a certain silence surrounding the subject, and the idea that women should either be shamed or celebrated for exercising this right. I felt no shame, but nor did I seek to celebrate what I'd done. I think I said this in my letter, which ended up as the lead beneath the headline, My sense of loss after abortion.

The first time I saw my father cry was when his mother died. I think I was ten. He cried again, a decade later, when a horse flipped on top of me, fracturing my pelvis in three places. In the hospital, in A&E, I remember lying on the stretcher, my dad, a doctor, standing beside me, becoming more and more upset. I was waiting to be X-rayed. He could see the excruciating pain I was in.

It was unusual to see tears in Angola. I think that was one of the things that surprised me about the war. I rarely saw anyone cry.

I've fallen off a lot of horses. The first serious accident happened on Prince Charles' and Lady Di's wedding day when I ruptured my spleen. In Ghana, sixteen years later, I galloped a racehorse along Labadi beach. It was a relatively small animal, but I lost control and it bolted towards an arrangement of tables and chairs where the Brazilian ambassador happened to be sitting. When I went back, on foot, to apologise, the diplomat offered me a room in his residence.

I lived there for several months with his Togolese butler, his Ghanaian housekeeper, his Russian girlfriend and his two Alsatians.

I have a scar on my right arm where one of the dogs bit me. I was stitched up without an anaesthetic. All I remember is the doctor making me laugh and laugh while he performed the most beautiful needlework on my flesh. To this day, I still like to roll up my sleeve and admire the wonderfully straight, wonderfully thin line of scar tissue.

Where is that doctor today?

When I was little, I used to play a game called Postman's Knock with my brother and sister and our next-door neighbours, who were all boys. I liked kissing Edward, but I can't remember who my brother used to kiss. Was it the boys, or his sisters?

In those days, my dad used to take us for barefoot walks in the rain and the mud. We had a large dog, who was called Franco because of the way he dominated our family. He was half Afghan, quarter Alsatian and quarter Retriever, and when he ran his long blond hair blew into the air.

Franco arrived in a cardboard box. I used to think this was how my father delivered babies – driving around in a van, dropping them off in cardboard boxes.

When I was living in Luanda, I thought a lot about my past and how it tallied with Angola's recent history. I was born in 1968, about halfway through its war for liberation. I was seven, nearly eight, when the country finally gained independence and the Portuguese left. Once, while interviewing a woman who was telling me about her husband's disappearance, I was appalled to realise that on the day she lost hope of ever seeing him again, we had been celebrating my father's fortieth birthday. I have such a clear memory of the party we enjoyed that day, but I didn't even know what Angola was back then. A type of wool? Some sort of sport? A fashion brand maybe? Admitting to that ignorance now is unsettling.

There was a period, when I was a child, when I began to wonder if I was, in fact, a boy. I can't remember when I stopped worrying about this, but by the time I was fourteen or fifteen I had begun to imagine that I'd marry a wealthy man in my twenties and that we'd have three children. I'm now in my forties. I've had an abortion, two miscarriages and no children. To my slight surprise, I'm also married. To a man I met in my thirties. He was living in a bedsit.

When I was a girl I was given a Laura Ashley skirt. At first I loved it, but then I began to resent it. I remember thinking, or knowing, that it was what girls like me were supposed to wear. Years later, when I'd stopped using a Zimmer frame but still needed a stick to support my wonky pelvis, I worked in a Laura Ashley shop. Because I couldn't walk unaided, I was sent to the stockroom to count piles of flowery frocks and skirts and blouses and pink cotton jumpers. I liked it down there because I could eat chocolate without being seen.

When I was fifteen, I remember telling my sister that it would be better if we let some people starve to death because there were too many of us on the planet. I think, in my head, I was thinking of people in Africa. My sister became angry. You can't just let people starve, she said. Yes you can, I replied. We argued on and my sister became very upset. I think she might have cried tears of frustration and because she was disturbed by my lack of empathy.

The first record I ever bought because I loved the sound – not because I thought I ought to like it – was a Pat Metheny album. I don't listen to it any more because it reminds me of a friend who went to prison for downloading images of child sex abuse. Whenever I hear Pat Metheny, I remember that man. I start thinking in a loop of anger and disappointment and regret. It gets me nowhere.

One of the best pictures I've ever taken is of an Antonov plane that had crashed into several rows of houses in Cazenga, a Luanda slum. I saw part of someone's leg being dropped like a piece of wood onto a trailer. All that remained of the plane was its nose and its tail, which looked enormous compared to people's homes. It had come down shortly after take-off at dawn, overloaded with weapons or canned food or soldiers or who-knows-what. A crowd had gathered around the remains. People were wailing and weeping. I remember doing a live interview from the crash site and, afterwards, being told off by the editor in London for being too descriptive. But when I sent my photographs of the crash to the Reuters news agency in Johannesburg, the picture editor said I was a natural and tried to encourage me to do more.

The truth is, I felt even less comfortable pointing a camera at people than I did sticking a microphone in front of someone's lips.

Working in different parts of the African continent for the mainstream media, particularly as a white British foreign correspondent, I worried a lot about what I should report and what I should not. Sometimes I asked myself what right I had to report at all.

After my friend was arrested for downloading images of children being sexually abused, we had a series of upsetting rows about the images society does and does not deem acceptable. I admitted to him that one of the reasons I'd left Angola was because of the voyeurism involved in my work. In the end, the two of us had such unpleasant disagreements our friendship collapsed. I felt I couldn't support him any more because he wouldn't take full responsibility for his actions.

Today, I feel upset when I hear people using the phrase child porn to refer to photographs of children being sexually abused. Perhaps I shouldn't be admitting all of this so publicly.

I think I really understand the phrase She's been around the block, but not the phrase For old time's sake. I don't think you should do anything for the sake of it. I'm not even sure what sake means. On its own, it becomes a curiously spooky word.

When I worked in Angola, other journalists sometimes laughed at me because I expressed my anger so openly. I lost it with Peter Hain, the British minister for Africa – the so-called son of Africa if you remember – when he visited Luanda. He voiced his support for a military solution to the conflict. This echoed President José Eduardo dos Santos' opinion that war was necessary to achieve peace. I reported this and later, Hain's office wrote to my bosses accusing me of misrepresenting him. I feared I was going to be sacked. I was ordered to send all my recordings of Hain back to London. A senior manager would listen to them and act as judge. Several difficult days passed before I was told I was in the clear. I still think about what Hain said that week, about the dismay he provoked among many peace activists across the country, people who'd lived through decades of war and who were pushing hard for a negotiated peace settlement. Just writing this paragraph, I feel the fury flooding back.

I don't think anyone who has experienced war, who has seen the damage it does to people mentally and physically, could ever wish for war.

As a journalist, I had some intense relationships with my editors – professionally, politically, sexually and psychologically. My best experience was writing for the *Irish Times*. My editor was a man called Pat Something-or-other. He let me explore angles of interest that veered away from the conventional media line. I believe that his sensitivity to Angola was probably a result of Ireland's war. Living close to conflict allowed him a way into the country that no other editor I knew seemed to possess. And it was a funny thing, in Angola, that the Irish people I met enjoyed some of the best relationships with local people. I think there is an openness to the Irish and a deep understanding of what it is to be colonised that enabled them to empathise with Angolans. For myself, I only began to understand the IRA and its war with the British government when I was living in Luanda.

In 2003, I was among the hundreds of thousands, possibly millions, who marched through London to demonstrate against the war in Iraq. I thought a lot about Angola that day. I felt very sad that there had never been a big march against the war there – even though, by then, it had already ended. In the public eye, some wars matter more than others. In Trafalgar Square, I tried really hard to squeeze back my tears when Adrian Mitchell read a twenty-first-century remix of his poem, 'To Whom It May Concern (Tell Me Lies about Vietnam)'.

On a Saturday or a Sunday afternoon, my mother would do the ironing and my sister would fold up in an armchair in the front room and they'd watch romantic black-and-white films together and they'd cry. I was wholly perplexed by their response.

I tear up easily these days. Outside Blackhorse Road tube station, three Romanian men were sitting on the pavement playing the accordion, the violin and the clarinet. Their music reminded me of the Cape Verdeans on Luanda's *ilha*. Was this a Romanian *morna* obeying the cycle of fifths? I gave them a pound and something within me juddered. Inside the station, the acoustics were perfect, like a cathedral, and as I descended on the escalator, I felt myself being swallowed by the sounds from the street.

When I started out as a journalist, I thought I understood the meaning of objectivity. But within a few months of reporting from Angola, I lost that faith and ceased to believe in objectivity even as a possibility. Yes, you can give a voice to as many sides as possible – but that's not objectivity. Today I don't even believe that objectivity is a useful goal. It's false and it's a lie and it doesn't help people to mentally engage in events taking place around the world.

I was astounded when I realised how television reporting actually worked. A BBC team was visiting Angola. They'd gone to a hospital to do a story about landmine injuries. Their piece showed the British reporter conversing earnestly with a patient lying in bed. In fact, the reporter was nodding and pretending to talk: the real conversation took place between the patient and an Angolan freelance interpreter, who was never shown on camera. The idea of the foreign reporter as an omniscient multilingual hero is a trick. I hate the way the news plasters over the rough edges of truth.

I was in my forties when a woman from Malaysia called Su taught me how to put on eyeliner. But at your age, she said, all you really need is a bit of mascara. Not long before I met Su, my mother had told me that I'd reached the age when I could no longer get away without make-up. Whenever I tell people this they laugh.

Apparently, I love Africa. I've been told this by people who hardly know me. I've been introduced in pubs, on demonstrations, in emails and on public transport as someone who really knows Africa and who is dying to go back to Africa. But I'm not sure I know what Africa means any more. I went through a phase of thinking that the word itself should be banned. Perhaps then people might be forced into thinking more carefully about what they're saying.

Not so long ago, an Angolan woman got quite cross with me. What is it with you? she asked. What is it that you've got with our country? With my country? Why are you so interested in us? We'd spent the afternoon at an art gallery in London, walking and talking and looking at huge pieces of work, and just as we were about to part, her distrust of me came tumbling out. It felt like a loathing. If she'd had a little more courage, I think she would have spat on me.

The trouble is, I couldn't answer her question. I tried. But nothing I said was quite what I meant. So I've carried on asking myself: What is it I've got with their country, with that country?

The only answer I've been able to come up with is that I was there during a war. It was an incredibly intense experience, one that influenced me radically. For a long time, I tried to work out how I could retrieve it. I wanted a repeat, like that absurd sensation you get when you first take certain class-A drugs. I was sitting in Shoreditch Town Hall. Duncan was holding my hand. I was thinking that my head was going to shoot off like a rocket launching from my neck. Get up! Dance! he said. You'll be OK if you dance.

Angola was a bit like that, but it went on for weeks and weeks and months and months – and I miss it.

Despite being forty-eight, I still haven't fully come to terms with being British and being white. A lot of people think I'm posh too. It's in my voice, my face, my whole manner. Even with my mouth shut, you can see the privilege. It's etched into me.

There's a primary school at the bottom of my street. In summer, when my windows are open, I can hear the children playing games outside. I imagine them standing in circles, clapping hands and taking turns to skip and jump.

One afternoon I was walking past the school gates with a friend. In the middle of a conversation about his new dog, he hesitated. Then he looked at me with an expression that reminded me of the first time we'd met. Have you ever noticed those gates? he asked. I stepped forward: I wanted to show him I was giving them my full attention. Then I said that yes, I had, perfectly, yes, noticed. But it was only in that moment, my Jewish friend at my side, that I understood what he meant. Standing at about three metres high, they form an arch at the side of the school. Each gate consists of a row of vertical iron rods, set just far enough apart to push a man's fist through. To either side of the lock that holds the gates together is a circle of metal the size of a small satellite dish. Inside each circle, a letter: M on the left, G on the right. At dusk, all you can make out is the top of the gates and the bare concrete wall running behind the back of the school.

When we lived in Bamako, J used to allow us extra time to walk anywhere because, he used to say, You can't go down the street without talking to every single person we pass even though you don't speak Bambara. We did try to learn Bambara, both of us. We took classes. J was a much better student than I. But in the end, we left Mali after just a few months because I was pregnant and had begun to bleed. I remember sitting in the doctor's office, half-listening to him advising me to go home and half-reading the notice on his desk discouraging female genital mutilation. He said he couldn't guarantee a clean blood transfusion should I need one. So I flew home, bleeding all the way, but having to pretend I was fine because you aren't allowed on a plane if you're bleeding – especially as much as I was. And perhaps I didn't really like Bamako very much anyway. I spent a lot of the time wishing I was still in Luanda. I still do. Moments when I get desperate pangs for the place.

OK, so I can't explain my longing for Luanda. But I wish I could trust it.

One of my strongest memories is the surge of excitement I felt the first time I heard someone use the word *camarada*, which means comrade. I felt as though I had finally arrived in a place where I belonged. I had a similar feeling when, after months of anticipation, the so-called fourth war erupted. The government began dropping bombs on the tiny highland towns of Bailundo and Andulo. Suddenly everyone in the capital – well, the diplomats and journalists anyway – seemed to be talking about the government's superior air power. I started using new words like Sukhoi and Ilyushin, which only as I say them, here and now, do I realise their onomatopoeiac qualities. If I remember correctly, the Sukhois were Sukhoi 35s – Russian fighter jets – and the Ilyushins were basically upgraded Antonovs.

Being an expert suggests that you know a lot of facts about a particular thing. I distrust facts, and the older I get the less sure I am of what a fact is. I know that I'm good at baking cakes. In the right mood, I can really get going on the dance floor. And I can make people laugh, sometimes to the point of losing control. When I put my mind to it, I can write quite well too. I'm fast at typing and very fast at sawing up wood. I'm also good at communicating with people, even on the telephone despite hating the telephone as a means of communication. But my real expertise, the thing I'm really good at, is being paranoid.

One of the reasons we moved to Walthamstow was because I knew so many people in Hackney I had begun to feel trapped. But now I know loads of people in

Walthamstow too. It can take me a good fifteen minutes to get to the end of my very short street simply because I find it hard not to greet people and chat with them all. I know several of the men and women who work the stalls on the market. One of them, Wolfie, runs a vegetable stall. We often trade stories, usually involving innuendo, which we both find hilarious. He loved my tale about the young fireman who came to our house when I had convinced myself, late one night, that our chimney was on fire. His boss, an older man, told him to climb into the attic to check for smoke and heat. So while J chatted to the boss and the rest of the team downstairs, I took this young fireman upstairs and showed him how to get into the attic using our ladder. Just as he was preparing to climb through the hatch, he bent down and asked me if I wouldn't mind holding his helmet while he had a feel inside my chimney. I burst out laughing and the poor man blushed crimson. When I told Wolfie, he blushed a bit too.

But we don't laugh about everything. Before Christmas, he told me his stall was probably going to be closing down because he was going to have his leg cut off – Right up to here, darling! – and I turned my back to swallow my tears. Later, when he saw J walking up the market, he called him over and apologised and asked if I was all right.

When I was still living in Hackney, I used go to a corner shop owned by a pair of Turkish brothers with large bellies. One of them was very funny. Despite living in the UK for over two decades, his English was close to non-existent. One day, I offered to teach him English for free. He looked at me as if I was nuts. Why you no learn Turkey?

I wasn't very impressive at school. The only A I got for my O-levels was in English literature and my teacher had such little confidence in me she said she wanted to send the paper back to be re-marked.

When we lived in Hackney, I occasionally shopped at the big Tesco's off Mare Street. One day, I was in there searching for ice cream. I was depressed at the time, and the store was so big I couldn't find the ice cream aisle. So I asked a member of staff and, as she replied, I could tell from her accent she was Angolan. So I said something to her in Portuguese. I don't remember what happened next and I can't remember what she said – all I remember is being swept with nostalgia and that deep urge to get back to Luanda. It was a painful ache that took days to shed.

The image of the soldier in M'banza Kongo, the one who put a bullet to his brain in the middle of the afternoon, returns again and again. When his wife arrived in the centre of the circle of people surrounding him, she screamed with so much pain it hurt to hear. She told the crowd that he'd been sad for weeks because of all the people he'd killed. What had finally pushed him over the edge, she said, was when the town was taken by the rebels and he'd been forced to fight for them. He'd had to shoot at his own men. To kill those he knew. And now he had killed himself.

I was invited for lunch with the governor of the province, one Ludy Kissassunda. We sat at a long mahogany table in his dining room, just the two of us, talking politics and drinking red wine. Years later, during my research for a book about a purge in the ruling party, I was told that this generous and gentle host was one of the perpetrators. Yet we had shared such fun at his table, talking and laughing and eating. After coffee, he took me on a little tour of the town and we were followed by lines of people as if we were dignitaries.

Six years ago, I sat with my GP listening to his story. Every summer, he goes home to Sri Lanka to offer his skills in hospitals there. Even at the height of the conflict, he went back and spent weeks treating the sick and the wounded. One year, the hospital where he was working was attacked. Many of the patients were killed. A dozen or so survived. My GP knew that they would have to leave before the next attack. But there was only one vehicle and it could not carry everyone. He had to make a choice and decide who to take and who to leave to die. In the end, he took the patients who were most likely to survive the journey. I think about the ones we left behind every day, he said, but there comes a time when you have to accept the decisions you make and let go of the past.

He urged me to drop in for a chat whenever I was feeling depressed about my experiences in Angola and Ivory Coast, and about the depths of racism in Britain. You don't need therapy, he reassured me. Why not give the *Bhagavad Gita* a go?

Briefly, I did try a bit of therapy. Six sessions. I couldn't be doing with the way she pushed the box of tissues towards me. It conjured visions of sperm banks. It's true, isn't it, that in the cubicle there's always a box of tissues as well as the obligatory mags? And, anyway, she was the one who used the tissues. Not me.

Lamenting the Consequence of War is the title of the first chapter of the *Bhagavad Gita*.

I wish my GP hadn't retired.

I spent a lot of my childhood on a bicycle, pedalling frantically to and from the local stables, at half-past-six in the morning and again at six at night. On my bike, I often pretended that I was on a horse and would concentrate really hard on seeing the stride into a jump. I didn't care what anybody thought: I was obsessed. I used to think a lot about John Francome because he could see sixteen strides into a jump at a gallop. I don't think I ever did better than three, and that was at a canter. Later in life, as I began to grasp the politics of class, I felt awkward about my horse-loving days. I still do.

I enjoy getting lost. I hate travelling with a map, particularly an electronic one with arrows to tell you in which direction you are or should be facing. I get frustrated when I'm with people who want to map routes in order to avoid getting lost. It makes me feel claustrophobic. I also panic in landlocked countries, which may be why I never really warmed to Mali. I felt trapped by the national borders. I used to wonder back then, if Mali was not a country and had no borders, but was simply an undefined area within West Africa, would I have felt less uncomfortable? Would I have found it easier to live there?

It is curious that the sea offers me a sense of escape because I'm afraid of it. I hate watching J swim in rough water. I also get anxious when I watch him on certain rides at the fair, even though his face is bursting with pleasure. I never used to be afraid of the sea. I'd dive into huge waves without a thought. Then, one day, on a small speed boat, crossing a narrow stretch of water to an island off the coast of Luanda, I began trembling with fear. I begged the driver to slow down, pleading with the other passengers not to encourage him to go faster. But none of them took much notice and the driver went faster and faster and faster. I was terrified – and that shocked me.

A week or two earlier, I'd been travelling on a truck with about thirty other people. We were fleeing the town of Malange, which was being shelled, day in, day out, by rebels. It's a long story, but during that journey I think it is fair to say we came close to death on several occasions.

I sat in the front next to the driver, who'd insisted that a white woman couldn't possibly sit in the back, in the open air, with everyone else. I was balanced on a small wooden stool between him and his wife, who was cradling their newborn. Every time we passed another ambush, the driver would ask me to count the dead. One . . . two . . . three . . . four . . . five . . . six . . . maybe seven or eight melted, charred bodies. He said he couldn't look himself because he'd have to make the same journey many more times and he couldn't afford to be afraid. He was a very brave man, that driver. I feel ashamed that I have forgotten his name. I think of him and his wife and their baby daughter whenever I'm on a motorway or an A-road, here in the UK. At the end of that awful journey, he told me that he and his wife had decided to name their baby Lara. For luck, he said.

Not long ago, I stopped three men from breaking into my neighbour's house. I yelled at them from my bedroom window, What the fuck do you think you're doing? To which they replied, We're visiting friends! And so a row started. Do you always use a crowbar when you visit your friends? The skinny one stepped off the pavement, looked up at me with a big smile, and said: They're our mates! You can mind your own business! I started saying sentences scattered with fucking and arseholes, although it wasn't until I used the word police that they began to back away from my neighbour's door. At this point, I charged out of my bedroom, ran down the stairs and straight out of the front door onto the street. I even considered chasing after them, but knew I wouldn't be fast enough. And even if I was, what was I planning to do? As these thoughts were tearing through my mind, the three men were squeezing into a getaway car parked outside Leonard's flat. The black hatchback was gone in seconds and, without my glasses, I couldn't even read the number plate.

Watching them disappear, I found myself wishing I'd used the word Feds.

Because I like it.

I got very excited whilst hitch-hiking to a town under siege in northern Angola. I was with a friend, an Angolan colleague, who used to make me laugh a lot. It was a peculiar moment in the middle of the journey. We'd taken a detour into some hills – I can't remember why – when the driver, who'd picked us up a couple of hours earlier, suddenly put his foot flat on the floor and drove straight at a pig snuffling about in the middle of the road. Everyone on board started whooping and cheering. We smashed into the animal with such force, the vehicle rocked from side to side. Then the driver reversed and we all got out to lift the injured beast into the back of the vehicle. For the next couple of hours, it panted heavily in the boot. You could hear the blood bubbling in its throat. When we got back to the driver's home, a sturdy woman appeared with a kitchen knife to slit the pig's throat. It was very impressive.

When my brother and sister and I were still at primary school, my dad used to take us swimming at the hospital pool on the weekends. He'd drop us off with a swimming instructor, an older man with a thick bed of hair on his chest, who taught us how to swim through hoops under water. While we were splashing about, my dad would go to visit his patients on wards with names like Annie Zunz.

One day, my father gave each of us a pickled pig foetus in a jam jar. I was very proud of mine. We all knew Liza, the mother. She lived in a shed behind the West London hospital, not far from Hammersmith Broadway. She was part of a fallopian tube experiment, but then IVF took off and that was the end of Liza. I kept my pig on a shelf in my bedroom and, later, inside a cardboard box with other odds and ends. Sometimes, when I'm eating pickled onions, the image of the floating foetus pops up.

I've never been more frightened than when we were driving into a village not far from Cacuso. We'd come over the bridge and turned sharp right onto gravel. We were going very slowly, perhaps five kilometres an hour, and as we drew closer and closer to the huts on either side, people began appearing, one after the other, raising their hands to their necks and drawing a line with a single finger from one side of their throats to the other. The driver looked at me: You know what that means? I shook my head. It means we have to stop, he said. It means UNITA is nearby. It means they're killing.

When I first met the man I married, he was living in a bedsit at the top end of what was then called Murder Mile. I was living at the bottom end. One Christmas, someone was murdered on my street. Bludgeoned to death, said the police, when they came round doing door-to-door enquiries. I felt guilty because although I'd been at home at the time of the murder, I hadn't heard a thing.

Shortly before we married, I made a ten-thousand-foot parachute jump. I wasn't afraid and as the plane flew higher and higher, I announced this to everyone else on board. So the chief instructor decided that I should go first. I thought this was a fantastic idea, but when the moment came to jump, I was so scared I couldn't breathe. I stood in the open doorway of the plane, my torso strapped tight to the man behind me, and just before we pushed off he said, Don't worry, I've only had to pull the emergency cord twice in my life.

The first time I saw people dancing kizomba I was astonished by its beauty and terrified that I would be invited to join in. In Angola, everyone seemed to be able to do it as easily as walking up the street. When I was in primary school I was sent to ballroom classes to learn how to waltz. Can you imagine? I have no memory of waltzing fluidly as a little girl, and in the last sixteen years I have failed completely to master the art of kizomba. I have tried a few times, but my attempts always make me aware of a certain Britishness that I loathe.

Another apparently effortless movement I saw in Luanda was roller-skating. Teenage boys would grab hold of the rear bumper of passing buses and trucks and hang on all the way up a steep hill that offered decent views across the bay. At the top, there was a roundabout where the boys would let go of the vehicles on the bend, spinning off at terrifying speeds, and then race all the way back down to the bottom. Sometimes it was pitch black: just the sound of their wheels running raw on the road.

Within days of returning to London from Luanda, I discovered that I'd made up words which I thought were real Portuguese words but were in fact non-words that made no sense to anyone but me. I was a fool not to write them down because now I can't remember a single one.

On my way out there, I was shaking so much in the airport lounge in Johannesburg I couldn't hold my coffee cup still in its saucer. So I smoked instead. Even that was quite hard.

I was promiscuous in those days. A visiting foreign correspondent from South Africa brought me a bottle of American perfume on his second visit. He threatened to take it back when I referred to him as white. I'm Coloured, he said. That small exchange still looms in my head.

Another journalist, a man I had thought of as a friend, locked me in his car. He began to cry and begged me to suck him off. Just once, please, just once. There is something awkwardly comic about this memory, because I couldn't understand what he was asking me to do. I had never heard the phrase suck off in Portuguese, so I kept asking him to explain again what it was he wanted. In those moments of unpacking the words, he must have known his chances were low.

On another occasion, the same man came to the flat I rented beneath the old slave fortress on the hill. This time he tried to force himself on me in the kitchen. But I kicked out and said cruel things. Months later, not long after one of his friends had died in a car crash, he wept again and while he was weeping, begged me, once more, to suck him off. I felt sorry for him, I believed his story, but there was no way I was going down that path.

I have had sex against my will twice in my life. Don't assume, as others have, that I'm talking about somewhere in Africa because I'm talking about somewhere in Europe. Somewhere called London.

On another occasion, a soldier held an automatic rifle to my chest and told me he was going to fuck me. When I said No you aren't! he lowered the gun and walked away. I spent that night fully clothed on the floor of a lookout post with two men. We were all bitten by ants, but my strongest memory is of laughing and feeling protected by two brave friends.

After the three men sped off down the street in their black getaway car, I telephoned our local community support officer, a very likeable man who was once Jamaica's national boxing champion and is now a published poet. Panting hard down the line, he told me he was in the middle of a chase and could I call back later? But the chase was a long one and by the time I finally spoke to him, a police officer had already been round to examine my neighbour's front door and to take details of what I'd seen. It was while he was here that I had what I thought was a brilliant idea. Another neighbour – a man from Kazakhstan, who once told me over a cup of tea that there's no such thing as a Kazakh language (only Russian) and that the British have always misunderstood Stalin (the Gulags were just prisons for people who broke the law) – well, he'd captured the whole thing on his CCTV camera, which he'd rigged up after a spat with a builder. We gave the police the footage. Which they promptly lost. Three times, in fact. I even received an apologetic call from the borough commander. But they are good officers, he said.

Once upon a Time in the West is the only film I've watched more than twice. I've now seen it six times and I've given a copy to two of my nephews. I was first shown it by an aid worker, an Irishman who taught me a bit about Irish politics and the history of Irish struggle from British domination. He looked after me during my early months in Angola, cooking curry and inviting me and many others to sit around his table to eat and drink and talk.

I went through a phase of finding it hard to talk without signalling inverted commas with my fingers. The words I 'inverted' changed, depending on who I was speaking to.

At our wedding, J and I each made a speech. I have quite successfully blocked from memory our performances that day, but I think mine was basically a political rant. I was still very angry about Angola's war and I wanted everyone to think about it. A man in yellow trousers filmed me as I shouted across this marquee full of friends and family. J was not happy with his effort either. We have destroyed the video.

A priest, who I'd met and admired in Angola, agreed to lead the ceremony despite both J and I being atheists. He said he didn't need to mention the G-word. Looking back, I wonder if it was wrong to ask a priest to lead a non-religious wedding. When we first raised it, he suggested we visit him in Dublin so that he could meet J and the three of us could talk things over in more detail. One of his conditions was that we attend a Bruce Springsteen concert together. And that was the day I finally got Bruce.

We had a pig on a spit at our wedding. I'm reminded of it when I peer into Leonard's workshop. He has the Morris Mini-Minor on a sort of spit, a long metal rod raised three or four feet off the ground that allows him to rotate the car and work easily on any part of its body.

Leonard is in his late seventies. He is rebuilding the car by following YouTube videos which he watches on two iPads: one fixed to the boot, one to the bumper.

I like to gamble during poker games and when the Grand National is on. Once, I made a ten-dollar bet with a brave and funny man that we would both be killed within twenty-four hours. He gave us a bit longer, a couple of days if I remember. As things turned out, we both survived and are both still alive, although we no longer communicate with each other. If anything has ever come close to breaking me, it is this. Everything seemed to fall apart between us after we survived that journey. I miss our friendship. I miss all the jokes we shared.

Whenever Christmas comes round, I find myself wishing that we all took more time to send each other cards during the rest of the year, when there might be something important and loving to say, and not simply when we are pressured to do so by convention.

When we were kids, my brother was Snap, my sister was Crackle, and I was Pop. My dad used to take the three of us on his hospital rounds on Christmas Day morning. He'd carve the turkey on the maternity ward, and we'd smile at Sister and eat Quality Streets and hold fingers with newborn babies.

Reporting on the conflicts in Angola and Ivory Coast made me aware of how difficult it is to distinguish between the imagination and what is really happening. I often become confused about something I've seen and start to question whether I have actually seen it at all. It's not simply that I start to believe I didn't see it, but that I start to think that I conjured it up in my imagination. This uncertainty plays havoc with my head. Something imagined is still something seen, isn't it?

I'm not sure if this is linked to what I've just said, but sometimes, when I see certain men in certain parks, I wonder if they are out cruising. I'm never certain. But I would like to know more about the syntax of cruising. And cottaging too.

I've been told that I'm a hardliner, a *jusqu'au-boutiste* – someone who pushes to the extreme, regardless of the consequences. I think wars are *jusqu'au-boutiste*, but it surprised me, both in Angola and Ivory Coast, that despite the war, sometimes I got a bit bored. Perhaps this was more to do with the nature of news reporting than the nature of war. I think that Herbert Marcuse predicted this – the production of increasing amounts of tedium through the evolution of mass media – in his 1964 book, *One Dimensional Man*.

Living in different African countries, although I've learned a great deal about the places I was in, I've learned even more about Europe, especially the UK and probably Portugal and France too. It was only after my year based in Accra that I really started to think about the double standards of European governments and institutions. I also became aware of my own hypocrisy, such as the fact that I haven't paid taxes in any of the countries in Africa in which I have lived and worked.

It doesn't take much to push a country over the edge, which is why I'm more surprised by the absence of war than the frequency. In Britain we might like to pretend otherwise, but our rulers are deadly serious about keeping control. Walking through St James's Park one summer, we came out on the south side, facing Wellington Barracks, where a long strip of dark green tarpaulin keeps military hardware out of public view. I thought about the Queen across the road – is she afraid of aliens? – and I thought about Jimmy Mubenga, the Angolan who died on board a British Airways plane just as he was being deported from the UK. When several hundred of us marched through London demanding justice for Jimmy, a man inside Wellington Barracks threw a plastic bottle at us.

I had never heard of Jimmy Mubenga until he was dead. Then, I started to think about him and his life, as well as his death, a great deal. What happened to him on that plane shows how far we have to go to overcome racism. I often feel very despairing about the prevalence of racism in Britain today, so much so that I well up. Yet, I also feel surprised when I am witness to it – as if, somehow, it was unexpected. In the middle of a troubling conversation not so long ago, I heard the question, How black is he?

And in the silence that followed, I focused all my energy into hauling back the rage. Then I said, Well how white are you?

I'm no good at lying, but I was able to lie when phoning UNITA leaders to talk to them about their military campaign. They liked to boast about their capacity, but sometimes they'd also feign a sort of humanitarian line or they'd insist they weren't bombing a town when they were. Once, I managed to call their bluff by asking them for the latest from a particular town. They told me they were protecting it, and only then did I reveal I was speaking from the place itself, being bombed by their soldiers. A dead cert for a conversation stopper.

My War Gone By I Miss It So is an extraordinary book about the Bosnian war. It's also about the author, a soldier-turned-reporter, and his addictions. Whenever he returned to London, his immediate priority was to get his hands on some smack. In Bosnia, his kick was the conflict. I met the author just a few weeks into my new job in Angola. I'd returned to the UK for my brother's wedding. Ant and I were sat next to each other at dinner. Before the meal ended, he turned to me and said something like, Wars fuck you up, you know, so be careful.

The only time I've smoked heroin, I was concerned that I'd shit myself. Or throw up. But what really spooked me was the sense of peace washing over me, despite being in a room with a junkie who was in a bad way. Old beer bottles were lined up next to the skirting board, the urine a syrupy yellow.

Is he dead now?

I became intolerant of friends who were still taking drugs by the time I returned from Luanda. I hated their self-indulgence. I felt isolated when I came back, and often unhappy. For a long time, I thought that leaving Angola was the biggest mistake of my life.

Sometimes, I'd felt alone there too. So alone I was almost invisible. But I loved that sense of freedom. There were moments when I felt more peaceful than ever before. Today, I am reluctant to contact the people I knew and loved there because I don't want to be reminded of how much I miss them. This is selfish, I know.

Occasionally, life catches me out. Like the time I was walking through Soho. I swung round a corner off Frith Street and there, facing me from the other side of a café window, was a man with whom I used to play pool in Luanda. He used to tell me stories about the cocaine trade running from Brazil through Angola and into Europe. I've no idea whether they were all true, but they were damn good stories.

Once I shared a bed with a man and the following morning, he pushed our clothes aside, pulled up a floorboard and pointed to a brick of cocaine. He put a finger to his lips: Sssh!

About seven years ago, I dressed up as Dr Harold Shipman, one of the most prolific serial killers ever recorded. It was for a fancy dress party themed Famous Doctors. J went as an old lady, one of Dr Shipman's victims. We spent ages choosing our costumes in the Oxfam shop on Kingsland Road. We sewed curlers to a shower cap for J, and made my beard out of a Father Christmas costume we bought for a pound on the market. Then we patted talcum powder over my hair to make it look grey. I painted J's lips bright red, and he designed an ID card just like a real NHS card stating my profession as General Practitioner. We were so convincing that people at the party seemed to disapprove of us. I think some of them thought we were both men, perhaps a gay couple. I remember finding it quite hard to engage anyone in conversation, so we ended up dancing quite a lot. Later in the evening, I had begun to feel so out of place that we swapped outfits in the bathroom. I wanted people to see me as a woman.

About seven weeks ago, I went to another party. The host was a trans woman and so I assumed she'd have transgender friends there too. As I was dressing, it occurred to me that other people at the party might mistake me for a trans woman. I felt a bit flustered, but J thought it was funny. In fact, somebody did get me muddled up. When you walked in, remarked the woman who was drinking Prosecco by the bathroom door, I was sure you were Jamie Lee Curtis. I laughed and told her my tales of not-being a Hollywood star, and of frequently being mistaken for a he not a she.

That evening, in that cramped north London flat, something got unlocked.

I was bitter when I left Luanda. Back in the UK, I had lots of arguments with lots of people. My temper could spark up simply seeing someone walking down Oxford Street in combat trousers. In the years since, I have fallen out with several friends for good. At a dinner party in Islington, I completely flipped out when a hedge fund manager told the table that the thing he truly cared about was getting clean water to Africans. I think something chemical happened that evening. I was ordered to leave.

What I wasn't expecting was the elation that blossomed as I walked back to the tube station in my World of Surplus camouflage coat, my empty shopping trolley in tow.

I was on holiday in Italy when American Airlines Flight 11 and United Airlines Flight 175 crashed into the north and south towers of the World Trade Center. My sister, her husband and I were visiting the Leaning Tower of Pisa, taking pictures of each other, our arms stretched to one side, pretending to support it. The day before, during an argument with my father, I'd said that it was about time the US got a taste of its own medicine. Perhaps then, I think I said, its citizens might start to empathise with all those people living in parts of the world that the US government has invaded directly or by proxy. I was very angry. Was I also very wrong?

I used to want to live in Luanda forever, with a revolutionary partner with whom I'd build a revolution. I'm a bit ashamed to admit that now. I mean, it's not my country and it's not my revolution. There's quite a history of people like me – white Europeans – wanting to build revolutions in Angola and other parts of the world. Who do we think we are?

I'm always surprised by the number of people who don't understand how I could have voluntarily left the BBC. But I couldn't carry on working in the mainstream media. I felt I was doing more harm than good and I was increasingly depressed about it. I think I have a true understanding of depression. Over the years, I've thought quite a lot about suicide as a way forward, but I'm not sure that I've ever given a full and proper consideration of the act.

There are seats on the Piccadilly line that breathe as the train races through the tunnel. The velveteen fabric rises slowly up two-three-four and sinks slowly down two-three-four. The first time I realised that the train was breathing I got quite jumpy. Now, I'm used to it. But a lot of people haven't even noticed.

When I heard about the death of the South African singer Brenda Fassie, my mind hurtled backwards at such a rate it felt like it might trip over. If you've never heard her hit single *Vuli Ndlela*, I beg you, address that right away. In 1999, the year of its release, it was played over and over in the nightclubs of Angola. No matter what else was happening, no matter how bad things were, it was the one track that could catalyse absolutely everybody. Or was it just me? I confess that in those days I assumed she was Angolan.

I don't like to think that Fassie committed suicide. Apparently she'd snorted too much cocaine.

In 2008, we were living in South Africa in the nice middle-class neighbourhood of Melville. A slightly creepy suburb of Johannesburg is the other way to describe it. We were renting what South Africans refer to as a cottage but, in this case, was a converted garage with a leak in the roof. One evening, our landlady's boyfriend threw some long firecrackers over the wall into the neighbour's garden. He wanted them to turn their music down. Explaining his actions, he said something like, I educated blacks like them during the struggle and look at how they treat us! The next day, I went round to talk to the new neighbours, to see if I could cool things down and also to distance J and myself from the firecrackers. A young man led me into the house. He showed me to a back room, where I was introduced to another young man sitting in a swivel chair surrounded by musical equipment. He told me his name. I'm Brenda Fassie's son, he explained. He gave me a Coca-Cola and I gave him a CD by Angolan rapper MCK, and we talked a bit about the state of South Africa and the fact that the neighbourhood still didn't want people like him moving in.

In 1989, I went to work at an *auberge* in the south of France. My job was to clean all the guest rooms each morning and to prepare the vegetables for dinner. The bit I hated was pulling pubic hairs out of the drains in the showers, but I enjoyed making the beds. A satisfying task. I like to do hospital corners with starched sheets. I would normally be too embarrassed to admit to that, but while writing this I learned that Jimi Hendrix always made his bed with hospital corners too.

One of the worst hospital experiences I've had was when I was pregnant in Abidjan. In fact, I only found out after I fainted on the way back from a three-day trip to the town of Duekoue, near the Liberian border. There had been a massacre and it had been quite hard to get certain foods and I'd ended up eating an awful lot of mangoes. I have a vague memory of collapsing, then lying on my back in a large hospital listening to the obstetrician tell me how much she hated European journalists while she poked about between my legs. With an arm between my thighs and a hand inside my vagina, she told me why people like me should get the hell out of Ivory Coast. At some stage she produced a long metal instrument which she pushed up hard towards my cervix. I thought she was going to rupture me, deliberately. My fear was fed by the murders of two other foreign correspondents in Ivory Coast: the most recent death was partly why I was there in the first place. Lying with my ankles in a pair of raised metal cups, I became so afraid I could stand it no longer. I asked her to unstrap me and let me leave, which she did. With J at my side, I waddled back to the car with a large adult nappy between my legs. We spent the next couple of hours driving about the city searching for another clinic. I remember calling my dad – by then a retired obstetrician – to tell him what had happened. It was silly, to call him like that, because of course there was nothing he could do from the UK. Eventually, J found a small clinic – it was a French one – and one of the first questions the doctor asked me was whether I had slept with a lot of men. It wasn't so much a question as an accusation. Then he told me that I had a very unusual womb. Like a large pear, he said, with a wall down the middle.

I read love poetry to distract my friend, Penny, while she was in labour in Luanda. The poems had been written by a man who said he was in love with me, but they made Penny laugh and helped her through her labour. During the last hour, I remember hearing her scream when the nurses pushed down on her stomach, as if getting a baby out was a bit like squeezing the last of the toothpaste from the tube.

Because I've been mistaken for a man so often, I decided – in order to have any chance of succeeding as a female foreign correspondent – to grow my hair. One of my pre-occupations, on arriving in a new country, was finding a hairdresser. One of the best cuts I've ever had was in Luanda and done by a French woman, a *coiffeuse* whose husband worked for the oil company, Total. Our conversation was conducted in French because, despite living in Angola for at least a quarter of a century, she didn't speak a word of Portuguese. She was adamant that to understand people you don't need to be able to speak to them. You just look into their eyes.

The one time I have seen J looking truly euphoric was when he took part in a flamenco class with the Paco Peña dance company.

I can't remember exactly where I was, but I was once offered a bowl of UN food-aid food, the sort that is given to children who are starving. It was incredibly rich and sweet – imagine Ready Brek with half a pound of sugar – and I found it hard to keep down. Until that moment of actually eating the stuff, I don't think I had fully understood what it means to be malnourished.

Cadbury's chocolate was one of the things I really missed when I got to Luanda. After a few months, an old friend managed to send me a bar of Dairy Milk along with a cassette of Islamic prayers she'd picked up in Kilburn. She was in the process of becoming a Muslim. The chocolate arrived in perfect condition and I ate it in one go while listening to the tape. A few weeks later, I discovered that Hotel Presidente, which was right next to Luanda's port, sold several different types of Cadbury's chocolate bars. So I began making regular trips to buy Cadbury's Fruit & Nut and a copy of *The Economist*.

The Presidente was a curious place. Sweaty North American men were always hanging out there, like CIA caricatures who would try to strip me of contacts over an uninspiring meal in the restaurant upstairs. Once, while sitting at a table late at night, I watched dozens of tanks and armoured vehicles roll out of the port and along the bay front before crossing the city and heading out to the zones of war. They were huge, monstrous things, and I felt very afraid. I went straight home and filed a report to the BBC, all the while wondering whether I had imagined the entire episode or not.

Begging is becoming common on the London underground. I watched a man – at a guess, he was in his late thirties – walk up the carriage and apologise to all the passengers. I'm sorry, I'm sorry, I hate doing this, I'm sorry. People looked at their knees or discovered a sudden interest in the advertising across the aisle. The woman sitting opposite smiled at me as she gave him a coin. I told him not to apologise. I kept thinking We should apologise, but I couldn't bring myself to say it.

The possibility of ending up homeless is something I

ponder quite regularly. I would cope badly with the cold and the damp, but I like to think I'd produce a good piece of writing which might pull me through.

It seems that the idea of suffering appeals to me.

I used to have this idea of myself as the sort of person who would be courageous in a war. I thought I'd be the type to put other people's safety before my own. A bit of a hero, if you like. But as it turned out, when confronted with the possibility of my own death, I discovered just how fearful I could be. I think some people may have been killed in Angola because of a selfish decision I made. I don't want to elaborate further.

I was on the telephone in Italy to my flatmate in London when I heard about 9/11. As I digested the news, I noticed in myself a sort of lightness of being. I'm not entirely sure I should be telling you that. I'm also not sure whether I should tell you this, but I've watched people being killed and later, reflected on the excitement I felt in that moment. I'm not saying I wasn't afraid or confused too, but an overwhelming vigour definitely swept through me. It was the same when I saw a group of children scrambling like rabbits into holes in the ground to hide from incoming shells.

I have watched a chicken's head being sawn off, slowly and painfully with a blunt knife, and I felt excited about that too. When the chicken had been grilled, I shared it with a friend. After dinner, we hid under the table to protect ourselves when the rebels started shelling again. Everyone in the restaurant laughed at us.

Not that long ago I laughed at a meeting in Walthamstow town hall because the two most powerful men in the room were called Mr Bottom and Mr Belcher.

Even when reporting from a town under siege, I've been overwhelmed by the need to drink two cups of fresh coffee every morning. Because of my addiction, I ignored advice to stay inside. But in venturing out, I learned the lengths to which many people will go, even in war, to maintain a semblance of normal life. Somehow, our habits and routines always manage to bob back up to the surface despite the constant threat of appalling violence.

The first cigarette I smoked was a Marlboro. I was twenty-one. I didn't feel sick and I didn't feel dizzy and I was on ten or fifteen a day for the rest of my twenties. Living in Luanda, quite a stressy place, I could smoke two packs a day. My preferred brand was YES. They came in a gold box marked with a red dot like those stickers art galleries use to indicate that a painting has been sold. At some stage, I had to go to the medical centre because I was finding it so hard to breath. A Cuban doctor examined me. He told me that unless I wanted to die young I should give up immediately. During the consultation he sucked on a cigar. If anything, this made me take him more seriously.

I still think smoking looks cool. I still miss it. And I kid myself that smoking may have saved my life. Cigarettes are a useful negotiating tool at checkpoints. I've never met a soldier who wouldn't accept a cigarette.

Now, in my head, I see grass as tall as I am and a red road stretching into the distance. Far ahead, we can see the explosion expanding into the sky. Another ambush. A coach-load of young army conscripts. I'd watched them loading up the day before, so cocky and excited about the prospect of fighting, boasting that they would be the ones to kill Jonas Savimbi. When we heard the landmine detonate, I saw my father sitting in a deckchair beside a swimming pool in Provence. He was wearing a straw hat and taking notes from a book with a gold fountain pen. There was an abundance of bushes of pink fragrant flowers.

Colette and Violette were sisters. They were short, although not unusually so for Mediterranean women of a certain age. Colette was the worker. She was also the teacher. With patience, she helped me get to grips with the *subjonctif*. She also trusted me with the key to the door to the wine cellar. Violette did very little apart from grind fresh meat for the cat each morning. She also kept an eye on the pet tortoise, and would encourage me to feed it the remains of the day's vegetables. When the sisters took me on special day trips, for example to the beach, it was always Violette who drove. In second gear. The whole way! But although they had very different personalities, they were in absolute agreement about the young Algerian man I'd met in town. He was not allowed to visit the *auberge* ever again. You could call this a turning point in my life.

The man who told me I was a natural, was made for telly and would go far, instigated another major turning point. It was a BBC training session at White City. I was learning how to make news packages for the screen. I ended my little report on Ivory Coast's war with a shot of two women walking barefoot away from the camera. On their backs, they were each carrying a heavy stack of wood. "Far from the bureaucracy of United Nations negotiations, ordinary Ivorians continue to be weighed down by war. This is Lara Pawson reporting for the BBC." The cliché was what he really admired. I knew I had to leave.

I wear a yellow badge with the words We Are All Migrants printed in blue. A barista in Salisbury pointed at it and laughed. A man in Finsbury Park station saw it and thanked me. A third person, someone close to me, said he hates badges like that: It might as well say We Are All Monkeys.

One of my regrets is that I didn't take more photographs. Although I was based in Angola for over two years, and have since travelled there for months on end, I hardly have any pictures. I don't remember taking any in Ivory Coast either, or Mali or Ethiopia or Niger or Burkina Faso. I did take a few in Ghana, but I sold them to a glossy inflight magazine. I didn't take any of the French sisters either, or all those men who helped transport us from London to Budapest. I tell myself it doesn't matter because memories of moments fill my head. But would I have more accurate memories if I had more photographs?

I only learned how to truly sit on a horse when I was told to keep my eyes closed. I was living in a hamlet in Somerset with an old man we called The Major. Every morning, starting before seven, we'd take turns to train on top of one of his thoroughbreds. The horse that really taught me how to use my weight and balance and breath was a blind stallion.

Yesterday, I was with a very dear friend. She said, without hesitation, I think I am losing my sight in one eye.

One night in the town of Ndalatando, we were invited to attend a dance. We spent most of the evening seated at a table at the edge of the concrete floor. We drank beer and talked quietly and followed the silhouettes of young couples dancing kizomba. There was no electricity. A few disco lights ran off a small generator. Shortly before midnight, for the final dance, the young women came to the floor holding red carnations. The flowers were a symbol of love, we were told, given to the boys the night before battle. But I have it in my head that they were flowers for the grave.

Where have all the flowers gone? We used to sing that at school, my sister and I. It was the seventies and that was a seventies song.

By the early eighties, when we were teenagers, I used to be able to make my sister laugh so much she'd wet her knickers. Sometimes, on the way home from school, I'd start making her laugh just as we got off the bus, to see if she could make it all the way up one road then the next without losing control. If I tried really hard, I could probably still make my sister wet her knickers from laughing today, but I don't see her enough and when I do, I forget to try.

In 1995, I hitchhiked to Hungary with a girlfriend. We made the journey in fifty-two hours thanks to a series of truck drivers and a silent German with a very fast car and a love of techno. Some of the truckers were reluctant to give us a lift. Rumours had spread that women hitchers were a risk because they – we? – would try and win compensation from the lorry companies by claiming, falsely, that we – they? – had been raped. In Austria, we got picked up by an old man from Northampton. He had collected food and clothes and medicine through a network of friends in England, and he was taking it to people across the former Yugoslavia. This wasn't a one-off though: he made the same journey month after month. I remember thinking how odd it was that anyone would voluntarily go into a war. He dropped us over the border in Slovenia.

When I was very young – about five or six years old – I developed the habit of sticking plastic beads up my nose. The sort of beads that little girls like to use to make bracelets for their friends, their mothers and their aunties. On a couple of occasions, I was taken to hospital to have a bead removed. Once, I'd pushed the thing so far up my nose I had to be given a general anaesthetic to get it out. I think my brother dared me to push it higher and higher. I think he used a sweet to persuade me.

A few summers back I had coffee in Covent Garden with a young Portuguese woman. She told me she wanted to go to war – to become a war correspondent. Could I give her any advice? But I'm not sure I've done enough warring to advise someone else. I'm probably in the category of toe-dippers.

And I have been a terrible coward. When I was living in Abidjan, I saw a man being beaten by government soldiers. I think he was being beaten close to death. I was standing on the other side of the road with five other journalists, all men. We could hear the man screaming, the whip coming down on his back. And we did nothing. We were in two cars, travelling into an area of the city where we suspected extra-judicial killings were being carried out. It was a weekday, but the roads were empty apart from armoured vehicles and soldiers striding about. We had been stopped at a road block and ordered from the car by soldiers. We had to show them our papers and explain what we were doing. The day before, the president's spokesman had warned us that he could not guarantee our safety if we chose to venture on to the streets. We interpreted this as a direct threat – and, certainly, none of us was going to complain about the man being whipped across the road. We feared we would end up being whipped ourselves. Or shot. Or who knows what? So we said nothing and when the soldier had finished looking at our papers and had given us the nod to continue our journey, we simply thanked him, got back into our cars and drove off. One or two of us may have looked in the mirror to see if the man was still standing.

A few minutes later, at the wheel of the car, J beside me, we came to a standstill down a muddy dead end. We were surrounded by homes made of brick and corrugated iron, mud, strips of wood and plastic. The carload of journalists we were following had managed to turn around and drive straight back out onto the main road. But as I began trying to turn our car, a crowd of people formed a circle around us. They looked angry. I remember thinking This is it. And I think I apologised to J for insisting we come to Ivory Coast in the middle of a war at a time of so much hostility towards European journalists. Here we were, months into our marriage, about to be beaten to death. Or so I thought. At that moment, someone fired a single gunshot. The crowd stood still. Another shot. They started to retreat. As fast as I could, I turned the car around and headed straight back to the main road. As we were pulling away, I noticed a policeman with a rifle. He had saved our lives. I have never felt so much relief as when our wheels rolled back onto the tarmac, but a few minutes later the fear really began to take hold.

The funny thing is, people often assume I'm sporty. I enjoy a bit of jogging and sometimes I do morning exercises – sit-ups and press-ups from the knee. Recently, I've really got into the plank. I also like to hula hoop while watching Andy Murray in a big game. Otherwise, my sporting days seem to be over. I was the borough champion over a mile at the age of fifteen. I ran fast because I was afraid of the other girls. I thought they disliked me because I came from the posh school, the one for Young Ladies. These days, I'd like to be able to sprint because if you can sprint you can get out of trouble. But I've had to learn to talk my way out of sticky moments instead.

One of the most powerful men I got to know in Angola was an aide to the president. Tall and handsome, he was always impeccably dressed in expensive suits. He wore beautiful ties and, so a Western diplomat told me, watches worth hundreds of thousands of dollars. Once, outside the presidential palace, he told me he'd started to trust me enough to call me *camarada*. He almost had me: I so wanted to be a comrade. But within a few days, I realised that he had just been flattering me.

Several years later, outside the presidential palace, the same man told me that my left-wing ideas were out of date. I don't think he realised just how miserable his laughter made me feel.

It's a bit silly that this still riles me, but one of the first questions I was asked, on arriving in Luanda, was how many A-levels I had. Then, what grades did I get? Next, what degree did I have? The same person also said that I was probably too attractive to be a decent foreign correspondent. A strange kind of put-down, but I remember thinking, What if she's right?

Years later, I found out from a man, someone I'd thought of as a friend, that he and a presidential aide had made a bet on which one of them could get me into bed first. Worse, is the slight pleasure I felt on learning this.

When I came back to the UK, I started reading books by Samuel Beckett. I had read bits of his work before, in my early twenties because I thought I ought to, but it was only after experiencing real conflict that I got any kind of handle on the man. The way I see it, Angola taught me Beckett.

I started to feel less crazy and to calm down. I say that now, typing it out at a pace, but it's been a long process. Although I haven't gone back to Beckett for a few years now, the experience of re-reading him – and particularly of seeing his plays – has helped me understand my response to war. The way I look at it, his books are rooted in his own experiences of World War II and the Cold War, as well as his Irishness.

At the start of the millennium, I went to Paris and sat in

a café just like the café on Boulevard St Jacques, which was frequented regularly, so they say, by Beckett. Except I was there to have a meeting with Isaías Samakuva, then foreign secretary of the Angolan rebel group UNITA. We sat outside and drank coffee and talked about the war and Jonas Savimbi and journalism and London. I bought a pair of long black leather boots for that meeting and hid them beneath my jeans. Last year I cut the tops off the boots so now they only reach my ankles. No matter! They still remind me of Lieutenant Uhura.

When I meet foreigners in London I listen out for words they believe to be English but are in fact made-up words that only exist in their heads. I like the idea of compiling a dictionary of made-up words.

I've tried and failed more than once to explain cockney rhyming slang to someone whose first language is not English. It's a hard task. Not long ago, I tried to explain it to a Brazilian friend. I tried inventing a sort of cockney rhyming slang in Portuguese by thinking of equivalent phrases for Barnet Fair, and Apples and Pears, and Boat Race and so on. I was going backwards from hair, which in Portuguese is *cabelo* – but that's of no use at all if you don't know the Portuguese equivalent of Barnet Fair.

A phrase that has remained in my head for over a decade now is, *Et toi! Tu es quoi, toi?* A French colonel in charge of an Alpine regiment in the west of Ivory Coast was ordering a woman to tell him which ethnic group she belonged to. And you! You are what, you? There was so much aggression in his voice, yet it was cut with unmistakable anxiety. I remember thinking: He's terrified, in the middle of this war he doesn't understand, far from his mountain base, in charge of all these men who are supposed to be keeping the two sides apart, who are supposed to be guarding this invisible border dividing the rebel-held north from the government-controlled south. Out of his depth.

Watching him was Yoda. Yoda was what foreign journalists refer to as a fixer. Born in Burkina Faso, he understood the conflict better than the rest of us could ever hope to. At lunch, in the French mess – I remember it as a large green tent but J says it was a solid building – Yoda made light work of the colonel's ghastly colonial views on the state of West Africa. It was a truly thrilling intervention. The colonel, half-hidden behind a flap of floppy beret, was defeated and possibly afraid. Perhaps this explains why, when I received the email, two years ago, that Yoda was dead, I wasn't surprised. Yoda is dead, it read. Straight away, I contacted J, who reminded me what Yoda had said when we had been afraid. What you must remember is they want you to be scared. If they can't see that, they can't do anything, so you must never show any fear.

You could tell that something wasn't quite right, even on the flight from Paris. Several of the French women who boarded the plane brought dogs into the passenger cabin.

One had a tiny white thing, all fluffy and cute with a ribbon in its hair, as if someone had stuffed a child's doll into her handbag.

Six years ago, I watched a bullfight in the south of France. J and I sat in the cheap seats, high up at the back. The rest of my family sat much closer, about three rows from the ring. We could just see the tops of their heads. There was a brass band – men and women in uniforms, veering between the jaunty and the melancholy. They began with something quite upbeat when the first of the bulls was released into the ring. The terrified animal stood before us exhaling sharply and I passed out. Promptly, a medical team arrived to take me away. I think the people sitting nearby thought I had fainted because I was afraid or upset – poor English lady – but I like to think I passed out from excitement. Once I'd come round, this turned into one of the most thrilling afternoons of my life.

When Jonas Savimbi was declared dead on 22 February 2002, I collapsed onto my hotel bed and cried. I was in Lisbon, on my way to the West African archipelago of São Tomé and Príncipe. I was crying for all the people who'd been killed in the war in Angola – by Savimbi's troops, by government troops, by South African troops and Cuban troops, you name it. For me, the death of this most infamous rebel soldier somehow served to underline the anonymous deaths of hundreds of thousands of others. The end of one man's life brought 27 years of fighting to an end. Pointless is the word that can't escape.

Two and a half years later, in October 2004, I heard another BBC journalist admit on Radio 4 that she had cried watching the helicopter carrying the dying Palestinian leader Yasser Arafat rise from his ruined compound into the sky. In response the BBC received hundreds of complaints from listeners who were angry at this confession of emotion. Initially, the BBC Governors' complaints committee cleared the journalist. But later, they said she'd 'breached the requirements of due impartiality'. Helen Boaden, the then BBC director of news, apologised for what she described as 'an editorial misjudgment'.

People misunderstand war and misunderstand death and they misunderstand the work of journalists. There's this big fear of our human response, of our capacity for love. Why do people always seek the pretence of objectivity? J laughs at me sometimes because of the way I express my loathing for objectivity. I shout at the radio when people are apparently being balanced and reasonable. I hate reasonableness.

Uncle Dick was a monk. He worked with Archbishop Desmond Tutu and Trevor Huddleston in South Africa. In fact, he taught Desmond Tutu when he was a graduate. He believed him to be exceptional. When people ask me how I became interested in "Africa", I never seem to have a story they like: I became interested in colonialism and racism while I was studying South African history at university. But sometimes, in an attempt to give people a more enticing story, I mention my great uncle. I tell them that he used to wear woolly mittens, which is true, and that he liked to drink Stella Artois, which is also true. The first time I went to Johannesburg, in 1992, I stayed with a group of monks who had worked with Uncle Dick. They were old white men with thin white hair who wore cassocks and followed a strict house rule of maintaining silence from breakfast until the start of dinner.

I enjoy silence. I need hours of silence everyday. But I'm someone who cannot maintain silence in the presence of others.

I've also stayed with monks in southern Angola. Fabulous monks. Generous and brave monks. They gave me red wine and told good jokes and we all laughed a lot. I've lived with nuns too. I'm thinking of the three nuns in Bailundo. One evening, a Portuguese truck driver came to stay in the house. Senhõr Meni. There was lots of giggling when he arrived. He was given a special place at the table. Over dinner, he told stories about the fifty-five-day war. I only escaped for seven days, he said. Other than that, I was there the whole time. I gave food and wine to two young boys who hadn't eaten for three days. Three days I tell you! Senhõr Meni's piggy eyes rolled at me. The nuns laughed. I came to Angola in the sixties to work and I never left! I bought my truck in 1968, it was built in 1964, and it's still going strong! Same colour it always was, Sisters! After dinner, Senhõr Meni went with the nuns to the chapel to pray. The following morning, he told me that I ought to pray too. He said he'd told the nuns they should make me pray. He said it was disrespectful not to pray to God when living with nuns.

When I was little, tucked up in bed, my mother would ask me who I'd like to think of in my prayers, and then we'd say them together, hands pressed flat, tips of fingers touching, last thing at night.

One summer, I took a train to Hampstead Heath to attend an evening of poetry in the former home of the poet John Keats. Among the many poems I heard that night, the one about cottaging in Regent's Park was my favourite:

> *All for the thrill of placing their knees*
> *on the piss-stained cold, the iris shimmering*
> *behind a hand-carved glory hole,*
> *a beautiful cock unfolding like a swan's neck*
> *from the Harris Tweed of a city gent's suit.*

I've never engaged with the work of Keats, but I like these lines he wrote in a letter about two hundred years ago: 'I am certain of nothing but the holiness of the Heart's affections and the truth of the imagination. What imagination seizes as Beauty must be truth.'

My tipple used to be Harvey's Bristol Cream. My dad kept a bottle hidden in the cupboard beside my hospital bed in Slough. It'll help you sleep, he said. He was right. Nowadays, I prefer peaty whisky and Prosecco. If it's hot, I like a lager. Sometimes I raise a bottle of Stella to Uncle

Dick. I also love lemon or orange squash. It reminds me of staying at Granny's. She used to bring us orange squash in the morning, with biscuits. While we drank and munched, she'd remove the potty from under the bed and take it to the bathroom to empty. I suggested to J that we might get a potty, one of those beautiful old Victorian ones, but he's not keen on the idea.

At night, before we went to bed, Granny used to lead us across the road in our pyjamas, to the large corrugated iron shed, so that we could listen to the rehearsal of the village brass band.

Another reason I left Angola was because I was afraid that I was becoming too thick-skinned. I didn't want to stop being shocked by what I saw and by what was happening. I was also feeling increasingly unhinged. I remember an editor in Johannesburg asking me whether I had my period. Is that why you're so angry?

At a party in Hackney I met another former foreign correspondent. He was angry too. A circle of skin beside his earlobe tightened whenever he wasn't talking and when he was, he'd switch into Arabic half way through a sentence. He kept saying I'm so sorry, I can't help it, and would promptly continue in Arabic. I almost felt sorry for him except that I kept thinking, You're ridiculous.

Why do so many British men still look to Lawrence of Arabia? And why do so many British men still look to

Hitler? I was on the train from Liverpool to the Wirral to visit my mother-in-law. A man sitting opposite me smiled. I thought he looked stylish, dressed all in black, his head shaved down to skin. I imagined him an artist, or an academic at the university. Perhaps he works at Tate Liverpool, I was thinking. He was reading a large book. It looked like an art book. I was enjoying the friendliness of northerners, reflecting on how much I like Liverpool. More people got on to our carriage. The nice man moved a little closer. We smiled at each other. Then I caught sight of the title. *Hitler's Elite*. Inside, colourful artwork captured the detail of men in Nazi uniforms, rather like the cut-out paper dolls in *Twinkle* comics that my mum used to buy me as a treat when I was a little girl.

He must have been one of those racist bastards demonstrating outside Liverpool Lime Street when our train came in from London. I wanted to assault him or humiliate him in a verbal fight, but in the end I just sat there and snarled in silence. I did nothing.

One man I wish I'd spoken to in more depth was the general who made it his business to let me know that I was under surveillance. His questions about my private life could only have been asked by someone who was reading my emails and listening to my conversations. Not that I much minded: I think I was flattered. It stroked my ego, that peculiar conversation at the military base in Catumbela. A bunch of us had been flown down for the day, to witness the weapons the government had captured from the rebels. We were treated to our own Sukhoi air show too. But the press conference didn't happen until the very end of the day when the press corps was pissed on the generals' plentiful supply of beer and spirits.

I was sober. I think I was also the only woman.

No matter how bad a war is, there is always enough beer. Booze is a good way to keep soldiers quiet even though it can't be good for their fighting skills. In Angola, rumours were always flying around about the use of drugs and potions and witchcraft. In Uíge, a whole battalion survived a rebel attack because the bullets simply bounced off their bodies. I saw it with my own eyes, the soldier shouted. With my own eyes.

I took witchcraft seriously then, and I still do. I also took military strategy very seriously. I became obsessed with *The Art of War* by Sun Tzu. I believed I would understand the rebels' tactics if I could just get to grips with Sun Tzu. I was briefly inconsolable when the BBC rejected my offer to write a 'From Our Own Correspondent' linking the ancient Chinese military philosopher to Angola's Jonas Savimbi.

Maybe this is something else I should not be admitting, but I took *The Art of War* with me while hitching through Angola. I told one driver that the book was my bible. It helped me understand the shape of the conflict. It was dark, and as we drove out of the small village, on the road ahead of us we saw the silhouette of a man. We jerked to a halt and the engine cut. Listening, waiting, we peered into the night. But there was nothing. So we started up again, moving slowly forward, inch by inch, imagining the worst. An ambush? At least we'd be the first to be shot. A landmine? Then we'll go up in flames. All of a sudden, this figure leaped in front of the truck, his face smacked with fear. Waving his hands, he ran to the driver's window. Lots of dead! You can't go on! An ambush! Please, take me! But the road was narrow, the truck was long, and the three-point turn seemed to last for ever.

Later that night, the driver asked me to read from *The Art of War* so that we might come up with a plan of action. I did my best to translate from the English the relevant sections on ambushes and sharp attacks, and then to apply it to our predicament. I believed we should drive on immediately. The rebels, I surmised, would be resting following the earlier assault. Our driver, however, knew better. Much better.

In the morning, when the sun came up, our fear ebbed a little. We waited and waited and then we heard hooting and shouting and whooping coming closer and closer and we could see the pieces of colourful cloth waving like flags from the tops of the Jeeps. They were from the next village along. The road was clear. For the time being, anyway. Last night's attackers must have retreated. We'd have to be quick, but we could go.

As a reporter, I found myself confronting very banal problems. Like how to put eye makeup on properly. Or what to wear. Once I was sent home from a presidential press conference with strict orders to put on a dress and paint my face. It was one of the most humiliating moments I endured. A friend advised me to get a handbag too. In the meantime, she lent me one of hers. It was yellow.

Closing on fifty and still no sign of a handbag. Unless you count my aunt's beautiful maroon creation. Have you heard of rug-hooking? Well, that's how she made it. I think I had that bag over my shoulder when I was mistaken for a transvestite. I'd made a special effort that day. I was wearing Spanish shoes with a bit of a heel and saffron red lipstick. I was going to meet a hip young Angolan man and a glamorous English woman, and I didn't want to appear dowdy.

I've given quite a lot of thought to Germaine Greer's view of transsexuals, that unless you've found your pants full of blood at thirteen you can never know what it is to be woman. Last year, I did find my pants full of blood – at forty-seven. It was New Year's Eve, we were round at friends and I'd forgotten I was due on. Returning to the kitchen, I whispered to Anna, the host: Have you got any tampons? She laughed. I've just come on, I said. More laughter. But, Lara, you know I don't have tampons – I use a Mooncup. More laughter. Fucking Mooncups! Helplessly, I looked to the other women in the room.

One was on the sofa, engaged in deep conversation; the other, standing nearby, a trans woman. What are you two gossiping about? she asked with a giggle. The pair of us looked up. I so wanted to answer her truthfully. After all, if anyone knows what it's like to find blood in your pants – the sheer vulnerability – it must be a woman who has undergone surgery to transition from a man. But all I could think about was Germaine bloody Greer.

The night before I left Luanda, a close friend completely lost it with me. We were with a small group of friends in a jazz club, downtown. So, Lara, in the end, it turns out you're just like all the other foreign journalists. Going home, leaving us behind, having had your little adventure!

On the flight home, these words played over and over in my head. I sobbed and sobbed and, as the plane descended into Heathrow, I was overcome with regret. The cloud was so thick and dark, you couldn't see the runway until we were about ten metres above it. I felt such a longing for the sun. Such a longing for my friends. For that friend. Why oh why had I come back?

Sophie was my first best friend. We would sit in the branches of a tree in her front garden, wearing long skirts and singing Beatles tracks to passing men. At primary school, I remember kissing Patrick and Daniel and being made to kiss a boy called Nicholas who had a German-sounding surname.

I loved Gary Glitter, and I wrote to Jimmy Savile. I wanted him to Fix It for me to have a pony or to go pony trekking or to spend a week with a pony on a pony holiday. It never crossed my mind I'd be lucky to be one of those who wasn't picked.

I was in a gang with my brother. It was called the Tuffies. He had another gang with my sister. The Tootsies. My sister and I didn't have a gang.

He let me use his air rifle, my brother, until I shot a bullseye and he didn't want to let me use it again.

Is that true? Well, I wouldn't want to swear on it. But this is . . .

One of the reasons we decided to leave South Africa was because I'd started to think about owning a gun. That admission makes me very ashamed. Fear got the better of me in Johannesburg. It was the stories we heard. Locked in a cupboard for six hours with your partner and two guests, not knowing when the armed men, who'd burst in during supper, will pull you out and rape you and beat your partner to death. Learning that your friend was shot at point-blank range while sitting in his car waiting for his son to finish Saturday football practice. Entering your nephew's bedroom with his morning cup of tea to find him lying on a blood-soaked mattress, a stab wound to his chest, his mobile telephone missing. Hearing that your father has been found dead in his house, having been knifed to death a week before by a junkie who'd been living in the roof.

I got off lightly. On my way back from work one day I was held up at knifepoint. I'd decided I didn't want to be afraid like everybody else – and so I'd walk home. Within minutes of leaving the university grounds, I was standing with my hands in the air, a large kitchen knife poking at my belly. The shorter of the two men took my mobile phone from my bag and I offered my wallet. Then the larger one, the one who was holding the knife, started shouting at me, but in a language I didn't understand. I asked him to speak a bit slower – What do you want me to do? – but he shouted even louder. He waved an arm towards the university and I realised that he wanted me to go back in the direction from which I'd come. So I turned and started walking as fast as I could. Within seconds, I heard more footsteps behind me. I'm going to be raped, I thought, I'm going to be stabbed. Instead, I heard the deep voice of a man with a French accent: They were following me until they saw you. I knew, the moment I saw you, that they'd let me be. He smiled. He offered to accompany me back to the college, to keep me safe. He was Congolese. From Kinshasa. I told him I'd lived in Angola and we both burst out laughing. We had lived in these countries with appalling civil wars, but they both felt so much safer than South Africa.

I've been held up at knifepoint at other times in my life.

In 1992, when I was living with the monks in Johannesburg, I got lost in the city centre and was confronted by a much older man with a dagger. I begged him not to take my money, explaining that I was doing student research on the role of women in the ANC and the National Party. Not only did he let me go, but he walked me to a bus stop. The other time was in London, in 1995, on the Victoria line. As we pulled out of Seven Sisters, a teenage girl, off her head on something, put a long blade right up beneath my chin. White bitch! What are you staring at? The carriage emptied of people at the next stop. Apart from one man. He stayed with us all the way to Victoria, when he persuaded the girl to leave me be. After she'd left the train, I thanked him for his help and he looked at me with disdain. I didn't do it for you, he said. I did it for her.

Nibble and Nobble were two gnomes who lived in the air-raid shelter in my godfather's garden in Twickenham. I never met them, but I was certain they were real. I had a strong sense of them as protectors, who would never let any harm come to me or Caff when we visited the shelter. With a bit of preparation, my godfather could do magic. All we had to do was rush around shouting Bananas! Bananas! and we'd find sweets under the pillows upstairs. Once, we found a pack of Benson & Hedges but they were for my mum.

I was excited when I learned, at a lecture at the University of London, that the Italian philosopher Franco

Bifo Berardi has a bit of an obsession with 1977. I do, too, though not for the same reason. That year, my dad turned forty, two members of the Baader-Meinhof group were found dead in prison, and a massacre of thousands unfurled in Angola. In Indonesia, it became illegal to tie in chains the mentally unwell. The British painter Keith Vaughan took an overdose. In his journal, he wrote these words: 'I am ready for death though I fear it. Of course the whole thing may not work and I shall wake up. I don't really mind either way. Once the decision seems inevitable the courage needed was less than I thought. I don't quite believe anything has happened though the bottle is empty. At the moment I feel very much alive. P.W. rang and asked me to dine with him tonight. But I had already made the decision though not started the action. I can't believe I have committed suicide since nothing has happened. No big bang or cut wrists. 65 was long enough for me. It wasn't a complete failure I did some . . .' At this point, his writing becomes illegible. He dies.

You probably know that in 1977 Chinua Achebe described Joseph Conrad as a thoroughgoing racist. But did you also know that, originally, he'd described Conrad as a bloody racist? I learned this from a really wonderful young man who gave a truly cheering performance as Manchester captain on *University Challenge*. His team won the BBC series and Camilla Parker Bowles awarded them their prize.

I have been told that I look just like Camilla Parker Bowles – in a photograph in the wind in Wales in my World of Surplus camouflage coat.

I wonder if she's ever been thrown out of a women's changing room. If not Primark, perhaps Jaeger. I say that not to be nasty about the Royals, but because it strikes me that she's another woman who could pass for a man.

At a dinner party, about a decade ago, a psychotherapist was discussing her work with transgender children. She spoke at length about Jamie Lee Curtis and the rumours that she was born a hermaphrodite. The therapist kept insisting that I looked just like Jamie and I wanted to vanish myself from the table like Samantha in the US sitcom *Bewitched*. But thinking about that now, here at my desk in Walthamstow, I wonder why it's taken me so long to see beyond the binary.

My new friendship with a woman who used to be a man is shifting my perspective. It feels felicitous.

Perhaps the most surprising thing I've found out in the last few years is that one of my relatives by marriage, Uncle George, was approached in a pub in Slough in the 1970s and asked if he would like to become a mercenary in Angola. The Cypriot-born Briton, Costas Georgiou – known as Colonel Callan – tended to target working-class men who were fit from labouring on building sites, but probably bored and badly paid. Uncle George's other strength was that he knew how to fire a gun. But Uncle George had no desire to go and kill people in a place he'd never heard of. He turned Colonel Callan down, which was a good thing, because Callan killed many people, including some of his own recruits, and was executed by firing squad in Luanda on 10 July 1976.

Shortly after we moved to Walthamstow, I got talking with a nice enough man in the neighbourhood. He was washing his car. One thing led to another, and he ended up telling me he'd been in the SAS in Angola. For a long time I thought it was a wind-up, but now I'm sure it's true.

At the end of last summer, I was watching an Italian create the most spectacular image of a teddy bear on the top of my cappuccino in the art deco café at Palo Alto station in Silicon Valley, California. An elderly man standing behind me in the queue asked if he could take a photograph. I was delighted and invited him and his wife to share my table. It turned out this pair of French filmmakers had, like me, been visiting Stanford University. They'd been filming a ninety-year-old scientist, still busy making discoveries and writing groundbreaking papers. And what about me? they asked. What had I been doing? I started to tell them about my book, the one about the massacre in Angola in 1977, and they looked astonished. Have you heard of Mário Pinto de Andrade, they asked, one of the founders of Angola's ruling party? Of course I had. What's more, I'd met his daughter and her mother, Sarah

Maldoror, who made *Sambizanga*, a cult film for anyone interested in African liberation history. The French couple were astounded. Not only do they know the film, but they have known Maldoror for years. As for her daughter? We knew her when she was this high!

I have it in my head that Uncle George never left England. He was born in Liverpool. He cycled ten miles to our wedding. He was in his seventies by then. He pedalled all the way in a dense wool suit. During the speeches, he got drunk and started shouting at anyone who'd listen, You're all a load of nobs! I wish I'd heard him.

He lived in a small flat in Slough. When we visited him, he offered us whisky in jam jars. I gave him the book *How to Bet* because I'd heard he liked a bit of a gamble on the ponies. He made a point of telling me I was a bit of a nob because I worked for the BBC. I admired Uncle George for saying to my face what others probably thought, and I was sad when he died a few years later. He was the first person to send us a wedding present – a cheque for fifty quid – and he encouraged us to give it to charity. And I'm wrong to think he never left here. He told J that he worked at Spandau Prison, guarding the man who was deputy to Adolf Hitler for seven years, Rudolf Hess.

Sixty or so years ago, Grandpa Robert was driving to the south of France with Granny. She'd run out of cigarettes, so they pulled over at the next village and she popped into the shop. When she returned to the car, Grandpa wasn't there. He was across the road, leaning against a fence, looking out across a field. When she went to join him, he told her that this was the field where he had been taken prisoner in World War One.

When I was about six and a half, I was taken by some friends of my parents to see a Basil Brush show at TV centre in White City. They were rich and owned an expensive car, a Daimler I think, with leather seats. It was so smooth and smelt so leathery that I threw up all over myself and the person sitting next to me. I can't remember anything about Basil Brush's performance that day. All I remember is the new outfit I was bought at top speed before the show. It was from C&A.

I still get carsick. In Malange, an alcoholic priest offered us a lift to the market to help us find a ride out of the city. But he smoked so much and swerved so excessively, that I was convinced I was going to vomit all over the interior of his battered old car.

Shortly after he dropped us off, the rebels began shelling again. We had to hide in the forecourt of a garage, inside one of those wells in the ground where mechanics lie to work on the underside of cars. There were lots of us down there, crammed into the concrete grave. It seemed to me, from where I was, that the rebels were directly targeting the market because there were so many people there. But, once again, we were lucky. We survived that attack, just like we'd survived the others. Later, we managed to persuade one of the truck drivers to squeeze us on board. My two Angolan colleagues were to ride in the back, he said, while I would sit in the front between him and his wife and their baby. He said he couldn't have a white lady up at the back. That wouldn't be right. Also, if I was easily visible, it would bring him more trouble. But I was afraid of sitting in the cabin. For starters, there was the carsickness, but I also knew that a successful ambush usually involves the people in the cabin being shot first. Your chances of survival are better in the back.

I can remember well the first time someone described me as a war correspondent. I felt like a fake. I dislike the label because it implies that war is something distinct from the rest of the news – that it is out of the ordinary. Yet, the whole point about war, I think, is that it is intrinsic to life. It is what we are. Britain has been at war continuously, somewhere in the world, for over a century.

I'm a bit hung up on Malange. My memories seem very clear, although I know I shouldn't trust them. It was there that I saw children burrow into the ground like bunny rabbits escaping from the bombs. And there that I saw a grandmother decapitated by shrapnel. I was standing about twenty feet away, my microphone in my hand and headphones over my ears, trying to remember the details. It was there that I saw bodies melted black at the side of the road and where I witnessed children so accustomed to war that they continued playing their street game when the shells came hurtling in.

Although I have come to understand that the violence of war affects families for generations, I continue to fear the apathy produced by peace.

I'm probably too judgmental of those who have not experienced conflict. But I'm probably too judgmental full-stop. That was the thing the therapist said that I haven't forgotten.

Jokes abound in Angola. A priest told me that my war reporting was defective because I never discussed Angolans' sense of humour. I still reflect on my failure to report all those jokes in all that war – and when I went to see Beckett's *Endgame* at the Duchess Theatre off the Strand, I experienced that pang for Angola again. It was that line of Nel's, the one living without legs in a bin: 'Nothing is funnier than unhappiness.'

I have a bit of a track record for passing out when I am overwhelmed. Within hours of arriving in Dubai to visit my old friend Brian, I collapsed in an Irish pub. I'd come straight from Ethiopia, from the northern town of Axum, where I'd been staying with an old woman in her cylindrical home. In those days, I had bleached hair clipped to within an inch of my scalp. My brother called me a Baader-Meinhoff lesbian. In Axum, the woman's son said his mother thought I was a man. By the time I touched down in the concrete hoax that is Dubai, my senses were overloading. I was standing at the bar beside a group of women. They had thick locks of bronze and black hair, fixed in position like warmed plastic. The four of them were looking at me, talking to each other, and then one of them asked, Are you a man or a woman? Minutes later, I was introduced to a man called Ian, who I recognised from a party in Tottenham, years before, when all the chocolate brownies had been laced with hash. This coincidence was the final straw: there, in the Emirates, I dropped to the floor.

The first time I tried to get a job at the BBC, I wrote a letter. When I heard nothing, I decided to telephone. I was told I could come in and speak to the editor for a few minutes. A week or so later, I was sitting in his office. He told me he preferred to employ people from Oxford or Cambridge. He said that, as a female in my late twenties, I was not an attractive candidate. You'll get married soon and then you'll have kids, he said. I remember telling him he'd not seen the last of me, but on my way out of the building, I had a real struggle keeping it together.

Two years later, that same editor gave me my first BBC job as Angola correspondent. I'd only been there a few months when another senior colleague warned me not to get stuck. If you stay here, in the same country, your career will be over before you know it. But I didn't want to go anywhere else. I wanted to stay put and learn as much as I could about that one country. I didn't buy the idea that you could be an expert on an entire continent. Before I'd even set foot in the place, another BBC editor told me I was definitely doing the right thing, starting out in Africa. That's where all the best journalists cut their teeth, he said. I wasn't entirely sure what he meant by this. Cutting your teeth is not an expression I fully grasp.

One of the decisions I found hardest was what to wear. Looking at other female correspondents, I decided to go to Gap to buy a pair of khaki chinos and a pale pink shirt. I had never worn these sort of clothes before, but they seemed somehow right. I also bought a short sky-blue skirt, which I wore for meetings with ministers because I'd been advised that it was worth showing powerful men a bit of leg. And I chose a white T-shirt in the department store opposite Brixton tube station. I liked the cotton flowers that decorated the neckline.

I've always had a difficulty with clothes. I remember going to a party at the local vicarage – I must have been about twelve – and all the other children laughing at my flourescent pink leggings.

At my leaving party in Luanda, my *despedida*, I wore a tight black dress that I'd bought in a shopping mall in Rio de Janeiro. Towards the end of the evening, another journalist put his arm around me and said, in Kimbundu, You came, you smelt the shit, and you liked the smell. That's what we like about you, Lara. Everybody laughed. But I hadn't understood what he'd said, so he had to explain it to me in Portuguese, by which time it had rather lost its kick. That night, another journalist said, Because of what you have dared do, I've realised I can do it too.

Not everyone was as generous. A man I felt I'd got to know well and who I still admire and love, said, The trouble with you, Lara, is you're just another naive white woman in Africa.

When I returned to London, I was surprised the night I realised I'd developed a fear of fireworks. I was also surprised by the number of friends who asked me how many dead bodies I'd seen. No one asked me what it was like to be threatened by a senior UN staffer. At a private meeting in his office in Luanda, he told me he could get me kicked out of the country if I caused any more trouble. Not long afterwards, I was at the Viking Club when I was told that my car was blocking someone else's. I went outside and was swiftly surrounded by three men who shouted at me for describing the Angolan president as a dictator. I couldn't deny it. Why would I? But they certainly put the wind up me and I lay low for a few weeks. It was much worse for my Angolan colleague. Men with guns turned up at his house.

Towards the end of a four-day journey driving north from Ivory Coast to Mali, I got myself into a state trying to defecate into a small hole in an expanse of concrete. I had half a kettle of water with which to wash myself and the concrete. Because I was not in the habit of crouching down that low for any period of time, the muscles in my thighs and calves weren't strong enough to hold me in the right position for long. I felt humiliated by my body. And I kept thinking that a snake or a scorpion would suddenly come out of the hole and bite me.

Playing in the back garden, I found a hole between the patio and the lawn that was probably about the same size as the hole I managed to shit into in Mali. Only this hole had a ground-nesting bee inside it, which stung the end of my toe. I was four.

One Easter, we walked from Bristol to Blandford Forum. There were few public toilets along the way, so I crouched down and peed in the grass instead. It was at the very end of the journey, during the last two or three miles, when we were passing through a village, and I felt this desperate urge to urinate. So I clambered onto the verge and pulled my trousers down below my knees. As I knelt, I noticed the kitchen window of the cottage across the lane. A direct view. I would have been more embarrassed but for the sudden sting of nettles on the naked skin of my arse and vulva.

J laughed and then he gave me some chocolate to ease the pain.

A Dutch couple came to stay. He had a collection of blades – daggers, machetes and swords – which he showed us on his phone. She was good at yoga and could fold down into a squat without tipping forward or lifting her heels off the floor. It's only Europeans who find this hard, she said, most other people can sit like this for hours. He said that I should learn to squat facing a wall because the wall reflects your anger. He said that when he'd tried it, he was almost thrown over backwards.

My mum has probably lied for me on a few occasions. But the time I best remember was when my brother and I had been throwing clods of wet loo roll at passing cars. We were positioned in his bedroom, about twenty feet from the main road. I think it was my throw that did it. Wet pink paper flew through the air and hit one of those vents that you sometimes see on the roofs of small vans. The driver slammed on his brakes, then pulled over. He was out of his car and stomping up the garden path in seconds. My brother and I heard him banging on the front door and then shouting at my mum. Listening from upstairs, we were petrified. But she told the driver that she didn't have any children, so there couldn't possibly be any kids throwing anything out of her upstairs window.

I have discovered that one of my main worries has a name. It's called the binding problem, which is the problem of how we perceive our experience of life as being unified. We see things happening in a sequence and we hear sounds at exactly the moment they appear to have been made. But the process in the brain occurs in different stages, passing from your eyes and processing there, then to different bits of your brain, including the bit that deals with memory, the bit that deals with shape, the bit that deals with smell, et cetera. With normal vision, and with perception of all kinds, there is a lot of unconscious guesswork that goes on. The brain knows what should be there and, to help us, it fills in for us, using unconscious processing and guesswork. So your eye is not the video camera you think it is. What we see is a simulation of reality. Which is why, if you have a damaged retina, and are unable to see properly, you will still see things – because your brain fills in what it thinks is probably there.

As I write, I wonder, are you, as you read, filling in words that your brain thinks are already here?

Once, I saw a woman cut in half by an articulated lorry, which was carrying food aid for the UN World Food Programme. It had been going too fast around a tight roundabout in downtown Luanda and had keeled over. I was in my car and as I drove around the roundabout, I saw the head and bust and waist of a woman and then, a few feet away, her lower half, wearing a skirt, her ankles and feet still sticking out at the bottom. At least, that's what I believe I saw and what I remember I saw. And it's what I have told many people I saw. But considering the binding problem, I wonder if what I say I saw was in fact fill-in created by my brain. Which bit was real – the upper part of her body, or the lower part?

And what about all the hospitals I visited? All those people who had lost one or both of their legs after standing on a landmine or running into a tripwire. I remember walking out of one clinic, dazed by all the blood.

The Celia Hammond Animal Trust in Canning Town is worth a visit. Cats in cages, floor to ceiling, room after room. While waiting in reception, I learned which brand of cat food doubles as a sandwich spread and which one a passable pâté. On one occasion, I had such a long wait ahead of me, staff encouraged me to relocate to the café two doors up. And who'd have thought? Everyone inside was speaking Portuguese, and the man behind the bar thought it funny that I could too. His face changed shape when I told him I'd learned the language in Angola. I ended up staying much longer than I'd planned, sitting at a table with several Angolans, discussing politics and cats and the difference between British and Portuguese colonialism.

Celia smiled when I expressed my appreciation for the abbreviation, CHAT. She said I was the first cat adopter to make the link. I didn't tell her that it was, in fact, J who had noticed. Nor did I tell her, when she smiled, that I could see the history of the catwalk in her face.

In spring, when the trees come into blossom, a memory comes back of a cat, hanged by its neck from a piece of wire in a tree in the town of Kuito. It was night time. It was dark. The cat's tail and its hindlegs were dangling just above the bonnet of the four-wheel drive I was about to get into. I was with my friend, Jen. We noticed the strange form just as we were opening the car doors. A group of soldiers came forward – I remember three – and they were laughing. They asked us if we were scared and poked the cat with their guns, which made it swing back and forth and back and forth. They'd strung up the cat for a laugh, they said, to scare us. It was only after they'd explained their actions that I felt any fear.

When the Angolan war ended, I longed to return to the country, to go back and see people I'd met during the conflict. I wanted to verify the stuff in my head, which I'd started to doubt. Eventually, in 2007 – or was it 2008? – I took a trip from south to north and further north, from west to east and back again. I wanted to check up on my memory. I tracked down a baker, who wept tears when he saw me. He said he couldn't believe I'd made the journey all over again. I found this extraordinary, the generosity of his response. Over grilled goat and cold beer, we spoke in whispers so that the spy over the road wouldn't hear us. You speak proper Portuguese now, he remarked, whereas before you expressed yourself simply through all that emotion. He touched my hand. We understood you perfectly, Lara.

The following day, a policeman invited me to read his poetry and to teach him the most offensive expletives in English. He was very funny. After supper, he suggested we marry and he took me to meet his sister. When I got back to London, I told a friend about this – she works in human rights – and she was furious. She said I shouldn't have socialised with a man who was implicated in appalling human rights abuses on the border with Congo.

In the central highlands, I spent a week with a young man who'd stopped speaking after seeing his father shot dead ten years earlier. His sister encouraged me to walk with him and within minutes of leaving the family home, he began chatting, incessantly. In English. If I broke into Portuguese, he would not respond. So we strolled through the town for a couple of hours, chatting away in a language he had taught himself via the television and the radio. The moment we returned to his house, his mouth closed and that same dumb expression swept down over his face.

Struggling to distinguish the real from the imagined, I also got in touch with a British man I'd known. He'd operated as a mercenary, first for one side, then the other. He'd dabbled in diamonds too, but was now a bona fide businessman doing government contracts. Ha ha. He happened to be staying in a hotel in a town I was passing through on my journey north. Knowing I was skint, he invited me to share his room. Being a fool, delighting in his kindness, I accepted the offer. It never occurred to me he'd expect sex – and the more I resisted, the angrier he became. What am I to do with my blue-veiner? he cried from beneath the cotton sheet. My response, suggested a friend during an email exchange some weeks later, should have been the Portuguese: *Teu blue-veiner? Não é vale pena!* Your blue-veiner? It's not worth it! Except in English it doesn't rhyme.

It was shortly after this episode that I moved in with the monks.

A few weeks later, on the outskirts of Saurimo, I waited at a truckers' stop just before dawn. I was hoping to reach Malange. I had a chicken with me. She was on a lead. Several drivers refused to take me because of the chicken. That I had been given her by a king made no difference. Until, eventually, a quiet man driving a white articulated lorry gave me a wave. So long as the chicken remains on the floor of the cab, he said. We drove for hours and hours through diamond territory, checkpoint after checkpoint, the chicken at my feet, the driver telling me tales of the trials of his life, such as the fact he'd fought for both sides in the civil war because he'd been captured by both sides. And I had three brothers, he said, slamming the steering wheel with a fist. Killed, every one of them. I was like a father to them. I brought them up.

At about nine in the evening, we slid to a halt. A wheel had twisted. We'd have to wait for help. I jumped down from the cabin to let the chicken stretch her legs and to give her a drink of water. Shortly, another lorry pulled up. Then another. Here we all were, deep in the Lundas, hours from the nearest town – me, the chicken and five male truckers. One of them began to tease me. Bet you're afraid now, he said, all alone in Africa with a bunch of ex-soldiers. You must be thinking we're going to rape you. Truthfully, I hadn't. Not until that moment, anyway. But what could I do? We weren't going anywhere, not until the wheel was fixed – and that couldn't happen without daylight. Another began preparing some dinner on a fire. And another set up a tent. It's for you, he said, unless you fancy sharing with one of us. He chuckled. His name was Cuba. He's the one I remember.

We sat around the fire and ate bits of grilled meat and corn and bread. The men drank beer and I drank water and I listened as they swapped stories late into the night. They were all from the south. They had no time for the government, but they had lost faith in the opposition too. They seemed certain they'd lived lost lives. They said they didn't trust anyone, not even each other. That's why we talk about acquaintances, Cuba explained, not friends – because you can't have friends in this country and you can't trust anyone because they might turn on you any day. He then stopped talking because he'd started crying. So much tenderness pouring from one man, it was heartbreaking. Someone passed him another beer, and he perked up. He told me he'd become a vegetarian because this job of transporting frozen chickens from Luanda to the border with Congo had put him off meat for life. You see, I trained as a veterinary surgeon. I love animals. Now look at me. Through more tears, he tried to reassure me. You can't trust anyone in this country, not even your wife, but you don't need to worry about being raped, Lara, you will be safe with us.

As the fire burned down, the conversation petered out, and out of the blackness a woman appeared. One of the men stood up to welcome her. He offered her food and water. Look at our magnificent Angolan women, said Cuba through his tears. They can walk for miles and work for days with babies on their backs. The men raised their bottles to salute her and then made sure I'd understood that she and I would be sharing the tent.

Beneath the canvas, we spoke very little, but we agreed, as we lay down to sleep, that these men were good and kind men and we were lucky women.

You know, I'd never hitch here – not any more, not in England – but I'd do it over and again in Angola.

There are some images that won't leave me. There was a bar, a small drinking den, I think it was in Kuito. It was a simple affair. A floor of dried earth. Basic tables and chairs. Comfortable. Clean. Despite the shelling, the shooting and the hardship all around, the man who ran it had no intention of leaving. He made a good enough living from the aid workers and the military men, who had nothing much else to spend their dollars on. But the reason I remember this bar is because of the small grey rabbit hopping about the floor, sniffing and scratching beneath the table and between our legs. It had just appeared one day and wouldn't go away. And this was how I came to learn the Portuguese word for rabbit. *Coelho*.

Uma figura – a right character – was the Israeli ambassador. Always dressed in flowing white cotton, she was old and manipulative and her hair was flame orange. She had a flat so capacious, I thought I saw ballerinas spinning across the wooden floors the first time I was allowed in. High up in a modern block with the best views of the bay, its white walls held the sunlight. Every evening, she conducted a ritual, serving homemade chocolate cake to a handful of select guests, two of whom were feline. We'd be invited to join her on her bedroom balcony, where we'd watch the sun sink into the Atlantic. As the thick red glaze slipped beneath the horizon, the ambassador would instruct us to Make a wish! Make a wish! Only then did she slice the cake, taking care not to upset her dearest cats whose prickly tongues were busy sculpting the chocolate icing. You don't mind, do you? The filaments of her face stretched to a smile. I always felt this was more a threat than a question and I never heard anyone say Yes.

The ambassador loved street children too. She talked for hours about the ones she'd 'adopted' and who, like the cats, she fed on chocolate cake. There was one particular boy who was so special she invited him to live with her. Occasionally we'd see his shadow moving through the apartment.

Then the day came when he was shot dead. I think she blamed the presidential guard, but I can't be sure. What I'm certain of is her response. She cried and cried and cried and cried, and her weeping seemed false to me. She always spoke of the president with such affection. She loved to surround herself with elites and power and money and men. She was forever holding parties and boasting endlessly about how close she was to Paulo or Manuel or José or Jorge. You understood that she was referring to minister X or central committee member Y and every now and then the president himself.

I never liked her. I never trusted her. And I came to absolutely loathe her when she refused a friend of mine entry into her apartment. She said he was drunk and dangerous but he knew, immediately, what the real problem was. I look like a Palestinian, he said, forcing a smile as her Mossad minder closed the front door in our faces.

Before she died, she sent me an email. She said she was disappointed that I had married a white, British man. I would have thought you would have gone for something more interesting, she said.

I travelled to the enclave of Cabinda where I met people who told me that an Israeli company was carving up the land for gold mining projects while pretending to be saving gorillas. I'd forgotten, until that moment, that the ambassador often talked about the gorillas of Cabinda. Like the street children, they made her weep too.

I was assigned a minder in Cabinda. He accompanied me for the week. He took me to a beach where mermaids come ashore, and he watched as I collected blackened sand in a plastic bag. He warned me to be careful when speaking to elders because often, he said, they know nothing about tradition. He told me, There's only one way to earn money in this province – by working for Chevron. The second best way, he said, is *Malongo Dois*. Malongo is the name of Chevron's onshore living quarters in Cabinda, a pampered paradise according to a North American subeditor. *Dois* is Portuguese for two. Malongo Dois means you are having a sexual relationship with someone in the army. My minder said that when he was a child, he would have been delighted just to touch a white man. He said, Everything we have comes from the white man. He said, The white man didn't let us have an education so that they, the whites, could stay above us, the blacks. He took me to a cemetery and showed me the grave of a British man, Arthur Galley, who died in Cabinda on 7 December 1893. You people have been coming here for many years, he said. He led me to an abandoned house on the top of a cliff. He said it was haunted by a mermaid who had been held against her will by a Portuguese man. But when I peered in through one of the windows, to the crazy paving indoors, I was swamped by the cast of *The Brady Bunch* and that song, most of which I still know by heart:

> *Here's a story,*
> *Of a lovely lady,*
> *Who was bringing up three very lovely girls.*

All of them with hair of gold
Like their mother –
The youngest one in curls.

I left my school 'for Young Ladies' at sixteen, with little desire to stay in touch with anyone there. On my final day, the girls in my class gave me a pair of gold earrings shaped into horseshoes. It was thoughtful of them, but I was just glad to be getting out. Two decades later, returning to London from Luanda, I surprised myself with an urge to make contact with people from my past. Like Della and Raphaelle and Emma and Eva. I thought about Mrs Teasdale too, my piano teacher, who had a heavy moustache over her top lip.

Driving to one of my cousin's weddings, Molly asked me why I had a moustache. They're big black hairs, like a man's, said my youngest niece. A few days later, I began waxing my upper lip.

When I was about fourteen, a girl in my class exclaimed, with revulsion, Ugh! You've got hands like a man's! It was at the start of an English literature lesson, and her comment filled me with confusion. I started trying to keep my hands tucked away in class. Sometimes I sat on them.

Size is a funny thing. I've been amazed by the number of men who really do worry about the length and girth of their penis. One man asked me whether I was afraid of his, he thought it was so big. Other men I've known – white Europeans – have asked me if it is true that black men have bigger penises than white men. And several black men I have known have told me, Once you've gone black, you'll never go back. When I married a white man, one friend, a black man, told me I'd regret it. And another man, an older white man, said it wouldn't last. You're the kind of woman who goes out with black men, he said.

I'm tempted to delete that paragraph, but there's more. Over rooibos and rusks in a South African staff room, I listened to an academic holding forth on the size of women's labia. She said she didn't like the sight of buxom black women in thongs and stringy bikini tops. She said black women are to blame for the boom in plastic surgery. She said black women with money have large labia which they like to have trimmed and tidied. I listened with astonishment. I was thinking about Saartjie Baartman, the Khoikhoi woman who was bought in South Africa by a Scottish doctor at the beginning of the nineteenth century and exhibited naked first in Britain, later in France. These vile slavers were fascinated by her protruding buttocks and extended labia minora. If I'd been braver, I would have asked this clever, skinny woman before me about her labia and what it is that bothers her about protruding body parts. And then I might have talked about my own extended labia minora. But I didn't have the courage. I felt too embarrassed. Instead I told her about my father, who spent most of his working life looking at the vaginas of women from all over the world. He has always maintained that women come in all shapes and sizes no matter their origins.

When I was living in Accra, staying at the Brazilian ambassador's residence, I was introduced to the writings of Martin Heidegger. The ambassador was besotted by the German philosopher, often bringing his books to the breakfast table. He persuaded me to read *Being and Time* and, once I'd applied myself properly, I did enjoy some of the chapters. But I gained more pleasure from the music of the Cape Verdian singer, Cesária Évora, who the ambassador also introduced me to. Regularly, late at night, he would return home from some diplomatic function and put on her album, *Miss Perfumado*, at full blast. After the first couple of tracks had stirred us from our sleep, he'd walk around the house, banging on the bedroom doors, waking each of us up, one after the other. Come and dance to this beautiful music! You must dance! Obediently, his Russian girlfriend, his Togolese butler, and I, his British guest, would gather in the main room and watch him whirling across the tiles, his arms spread wide, his fingers clicking.

The following year, Robert, the butler, emailed me from the ambassador's new residence in the Mozambican capital, Maputo. He'd heard my World Service radio reports from Angola and couldn't believe it was actually me. The ambassador was still dancing at midnight, he said. The dogs were still alive.

It disappoints me that I have become the kind of person who is afraid of certain dogs. Franco was a very large dog and he never bit anyone. But Prince, the larger of the ambassador's two Alsatians, frightened me. He lived on the roof of the Accra residence with his little sister Baleia, which is the Portuguese word for whale. Every morning it was Robert's job to bring the dogs through the house and release them into the yard so that they could roam around the gardens. He would always warn me when they were coming down so I that could shut myself into my room.

The last time we spoke, Robert was living in the US, a contented man from what I could gather.

While queueing at the the post office, I was telling the man behind me about the dogs that have chased me when I've been out running on the marshes. It's the men you should be worried about, he replied. There've been some very nasty attacks down there and one woman even got raped. Indeed, I did know about this, but I told him that it wouldn't stop me running. I won't have my life shaped by the possibility that I might be attacked by some strange man, I said. Everyone else in the queue was listening, including the post office staff. No one said a word.

In another queue at the same post office, I turned round when I heard a woman say sternly: I know what you're doing and I want it to stop immediately! Two middle-aged men looked up. One of them curled his top lip into a sneer, and his friend put a hand over his mouth as his shoulders started shaking. Stop it! she said a second time. Further up the queue, another man straightened his back. His thinning hair was knotted into a bun at the base of his head. He wore large sunglasses that covered his cheeks, and a fitted polo-necked jumper which emphasised his long neck and slim upper body, reminding me of the Canada geese that breed by the reservoirs on Coppermill Lane. On his feet, a pair of leather ankle boots with a neat mid-height heel, like the flamenco dancer who left me gasping when he charged like a stallion on to the stage in a club in the Albaicín in Granada. Over his dark trousers, here, in Walthamstow, he wore a skirt and he had a guitar strapped to his back. Everybody else in the queue was pretending not to look, including the post office staff. I was openly staring. None of us said a word.

I had nylon sheets when I was a child. They were turquoise. I had nylon pyjamas too. My mum told me that only miners' children wore their pants and vests in bed.

When I left home just before my seventeenth birthday, I lived in a half-built house in a hamlet in Somerset. The windows were of thin glass, there was no central heating, and it was absolutely freezing. I used to go to bed in the clothes I wore during the day, including my gloves and, in the depths of the winter, a woolly hat too. I'd shower once a fortnight. Getting undressed was a horrible experience.

I was living with an elderly man who dowsed with a pendulum of crystal. He taught me how to dowse too. My pendulum was made of copper. The Major was one of the people I wanted to see when I returned from Angola in 2001. So I drove down to Somerset, alone. He didn't look any older despite the years that had passed, however he did have a cancerous tumour in his head. As he showed me around the farm yard, he spat into a pudding bowl which he held with both hands, and I could see the thick yellow pus swilling around inside. He told me he was treating himself with dowsing and radionics. He said there was only so much the hospital could do.

Every year, J makes Christmas puddings for my family and his family, and for our friends and a few of the neighbours too. The pudding bowls he uses are the same as the Major's.

For my first Christmas in Luanda, I was invited to celebrate with the family whose room I was renting. The kitchen table was covered with large cakes on china plates, and lots of people came by. Among the presents that were given, my landlady's thirteen-year-old son received a packet of condoms – from his mother. Everyone thought it very amusing and very British that I was so shocked. There was a lot of laughter that day.

A man I thought I was in love with refused to use a condom. Lying on the bed in Luanda, he said it was un-African and insisted that the Pope was trying to stunt the growth of the African population. I didn't argue. It wasn't that I agreed or disagreed, but that the war had made me alert to life. I wasn't afraid of death. I wanted to enjoy myself there and then, in that moment, while I was lucky enough to have it. Two years later, in London, an Angolan friend told me I deserved to get HIV. You're a foolish European playing with the idea of death, he said.

I worried about HIV during a ride in an Antonov plane. In the cockpit, the pair of Ukrainian pilots were taking it in turns to swig from a bottle of vodka. They offered me a swig too. How could I complain? They were giving me a free lift. I thanked them and took a quick gulp. After take-off, they were asked to divert to the north to pick up some injured soldiers. We landed on a short airstrip close to the Congo border about an hour later. The rear cargo ramp was lowered and perhaps a dozen soldiers on stretchers were rushed on board. They had thick needles in their arms, and their drips were quickly clipped to bits of metal work on the ceiling of the plane. The rear ramp was then closed again and we taxied back down the runway. We turned to take off and, as the aircraft accelerated, so the stretchers began to move. The faster we went, the further they slid. And the further they slid, the more the rubber tubes stretched – from the drips fixed to the ceiling to the needles in the men's arms. I can't remember who else was on board, but each of us tried to hold on to at least one stretcher. There was a lot of blood. The men were very sick. We did our best.

I loved those plane journeys. They were nerve-racking but thrilling. Each time we landed in another battered airport, I delighted in having made it again. Of course, there were crashes. We all knew that. But the number of bashed up old Antonovs that kept on chugging through the skies, missing missiles and bumping down onto broken runways – it really was something.

I was ill-prepared for the job. I hardly spoke a word of Portuguese, let alone any Angolan language. I used to record the state radio news bulletins and then, with the dictionary open, would spend ages trying to translate the details. Sometimes I'd have to ask my landlady's son, or her cleaner, to explain a particular phrase. Several of the local journalists were also very generous with their knowledge. Even so, at the beginning, because my Portuguese was so poor, there were times when I struggled to believe what I heard. I thought I must have misunderstood. It couldn't possibly be true.

During a bombing raid, I was told that the locals called the shells by the male name João. My friend told me to listen more carefully when they came hurtling towards us. You see? You see! Jjjjjj-WOW.

Years later, Inácio came to stay for Christmas. Together, we looked through the windows of the Ecuadorian embassy hoping for a glimpse of Julian Assange. Then I took him to see the food hall at Harrods, and we got talking with a young Congolese man who was working on the chocolate counter. Outside, a big Scot in a kilt was playing the bagpipes. Inácio stood beside him. They put their arms around each other and I took a photograph. It was strange, in that moment, thinking about the 1983 Harrods bombing on that same spot. I remember because my brother had a holiday job as a porter at Harrods. My mum was frantic with worry. Staring at the Scot, his arm wrapped round my friend's shoulder, I thought about the shells called João in Malange.

I wanted Inácio to understand just how corrupt Britain is, so I took him on a little tour of the City of London. We also went to Westminster to look at Big Ben – and Churchill and Gandhi, Mandela and Rhodes. Again it was strange standing in front of Cecil Rhodes' enormous statue with my Angolan friend, but Inácio enjoyed Westminster so much he insisted on a return trip a few days later. On Christmas Day, we drove to my brother's house in the New Forest and on Boxing Day afternoon, in heavy rain, we stood with our fingers curled into a wire fence and stared at Stonehenge.

People tend not to believe me when I tell them that my mum sent me to primary school with the ends of my shoes cut off, leaving my toes poking out in white socks. They'll be fine for the summer, she said.

The first time I used a tampon, I felt like I was trying to reinsert an expanded cork into a bottle of wine. We were in the south of France. I didn't have a clue. And the whole thing made me hate being female. I often wondered, in Angola, how women living far from shops and medical clinics coped each month. Where did they get their sanitary towels and their tampons? What did they do? What did they use? Why didn't I ever try to make a programme about it? I never even enquired.

These days, I nearly always carry tampons on me, just in case I meet another woman who's been caught out. In the bushes at the side of the road, I had the opportunity to help a woman during a demonstration against the Heathrow third runway. Can you imagine being kettled outside Westminster and coming on? I'm not saying worse things don't happen.

The first time I travelled to Luanda I took loads of tampons. Looking back, I think this says a lot about my perception of the country at the time. My ignorance. That my bra and knickers were stuffed with thousands of US dollars was less foolish. That was absolutely necessary.

The first time I used a Mooncup, it was New Year's Eve and I was becoming steadily drunk. Folding then pushing in the silicone goblet, my mind was elsewhere. I was frustrated to be missing out on the conversations downstairs. It wasn't until the following morning that I realised I didn't know how I was going to retrieve it. I'd snipped its stalk in a hurry, leaving just half a centimetre poking out. The instructions discourage panic. If you can't feel the stalk, sit on the toilet, relax and start pushing. It took me close to twenty minutes to get a good enough grip, and during the final tug I imagined my entire womb being sucked out.

On separate occasions, on separate streets, in separate parts of London, a neighbour has called me to tell me that her partner has just attacked her and she's afraid and can she come over. The first time this happened, a pair of psychoanalysts reassured the terrified woman that it was perfectly normal for couples to hit each other every now and then. The second time, I picked up my umbrella and went round to confront the man myself. I was a bit scared, but I knew that if I followed Yoda's advice and showed no fear, I'd be fine. And it worked. I told the violent boyfriend he had to leave the house. He told me it was her fault, that she liked making him do it. Later that day, he did leave the house. Later that week, he came back.

I've been hit by a boyfriend once in my life, and I hit that one back. J says it's good I'm not a man. He says that if I was I'd have been locked up by now.

When I heard a teenage boy outside my gate talking about getting a gun, I exploded. I stormed into the road and yelled at him. He looked horrified. I didn't say nothing about a gun! I didn't, I didn't! But I didn't believe him. I told him he'd be the one who'll end up being shot if he gets involved with guns. I told him to take a long hard look at his life. But he was taking a long hard look at me, like I was a lunatic. He pulled his bike up from the pavement and sped off down the street.

Often, I regret it when I've shouted at kids around here. Sometimes, I try to find them to apologise. One guy – he was about seventeen – told me not to worry. We all lose our temper, he said. But I still felt bad that I'd sworn at him. He said he thought it was funny and now, when we see each other, we always say hello. Sometimes he walks with me.

I came home to find a group of lads and their Staffie huddled around our back gate. One of them was urinating on it. I lost it. Would you piss on your mother's back gate? Or your sister's? They all turned round. The one who'd been pissing was trying to tuck his cock away. I kept on shouting. I don't want your fucking piss all over my gate! It stinks! Why can't you piss down the fucking drain? There was an embarrassed silence. Almost comic. Then a larger lad turned to his friend and told him that I was making a fair point. He sent him off. Then he invited me to meet the dog. It was a really friendly dog. I liked it and I think it liked me. A few minutes later, the guy came back with a bucket of soapy water. He washed the gate carefully. Again, I found myself apologising for shouting so loudly, to which one of them piped up: You've probably woken up your neighbours, what with all that swearing.

When I was on a Zimmer frame, I noticed that people treated me as if I had a mental disability not a physical one. I remember standing beside my dad in Windsor town centre and this woman talking to him about me. It was as if I wasn't there. I thought about this, years later, during a press conference in Bamako. The only journalists who were invited to ask questions of Colonel Gaddafi were male. My raised hand was invisible.

When I came back to the UK, certain things stood out, things I'd not noticed before. Such as the similarity between our supermarkets and our churches, between our malls and our cathedrals. In Kingston upon Thames, I had a duck-rabbit moment at The Bentall Centre. This was followed by a wave of excitement, similar to my experience at the bullfight in France. I had to sit down, to take the necessary time to digest my surroundings, to slow the spinning.

In 1998, when I was shown around Luanda for the first time, my predecessor took me to see Agostinho Neto's mausoleum. Neto was Angola's first president until his death in 1979. The mausoleum is a giant grey projectile that has never taken off. As we sat staring at it, the red car rumbling in neutral, the woman beside me said I was looking at Angola's space rocket project. I believed her.

That mausoleum occupies the same cells in my brain as the climb-in Dalek we briefly looked after in Sheen.

Five months in and I became so depressed by all the death and the extraordinary suffering that I decided to stop killing the cockroaches in my room. One day, a priest popped in to see me. There were three large roaches flying about. He advised me to get some spray, that stuff that comes in a big blue and white bottle and acts like superglue. When I said I couldn't stand any more death, he told me to get over it.

When Charly was about to be deported from Britain, I begged him not to struggle on board the plane. I was afraid he would die, like Jimmy Mubenga. I had tried, and failed, to help Charly. As a child, he was brought to London from Kinshasa by his father. As a teenager, he made a foolish mistake and was sent to prison. By the time he came out, he had lost the right to remain here. Together, we found a solicitor who tried, and failed, to help him. The solicitor's father had been friends with Holden Roberto, one of Angola's liberation leaders. We shared a rushed but interesting discussion in his cramped office on Green Lanes, and Charly was sent home anyway. Except Kinshasa wasn't home. He knew no one there. His grandmother had died and his mother was living in Cabinda. She is the reason Charly and I met. She had taken good care of me when I visited Cabinda in 2008. She took me to the market and on a tour of the city. Shortly before I flew out, she asked me if I could try to find her son. He's in prison in London, she said. He was living in a place called Tottingham, she said. It took me several months to track down Charly. But I got there, in the end, thanks to an Angola-Congo network in north London. Charly was living in Tottenham, a couple of miles away from me. Is that what you'd call a coincidence?

To mend my broken pelvis, the doctors drilled a hole through my left shinbone just below the knee. Then they hammered a stainless steel skewer through it. Wires ran from either end of the skewer down the length of my lower leg to a pulley system which was attached to the end of the bed. Hanging beneath the pulley was a lead weight the size of a salmon. In the next bed lay an elderly woman who had Alzheimer's. She'd broken her wrist and bruised her thigh, but was able to walk. One night, she climbed out of bed and briefly vanished from the ward. When she returned, she was holding a plastic basin. She pulled up her nightie, held the basin between her legs, and pissed into it. When she'd finished, she placed the basin on the floor and undressed. She placed her nightie inside the basin, pushing it into the urine. Then she picked up the basin and walked towards me. She placed it beside me on the bed and began to knead her nightdress, as if she was washing it in wee.

The pain of my fractured pelvis kept me awake. So did other patients. And I spent an entire night on a bedpan desperate to defecate. The nurse said I couldn't have been in more agony if I'd been giving birth. Another time, I couldn't fall asleep because I was too scared. A dangerous man was on the loose, searching the wards for the wife he had brutally attacked that day.

I suffered from insomnia when I was writing my book about the 1977 massacre in Angola. I was drowning in anxiety. There was a phase when I used to wake in the middle of the night in absolute panic. I'd sit in a sweat on the edge of the bed, overwhelmed by the prospect of failure, unable to relax for hours. J was incredible. Patient doesn't even get close. He taught me all sorts of tricks, ways to empty my mind of negative thoughts even in the middle of the night. Looking back, it's hard to understand how I could have been so afraid of something that could never kill me. Although, failure is more frightening than death.

You have to endure it.

Is it psychological or physical? I become very anxious when I'm in an enclosed space watching couples dancing kizomba. There's a kind of anger at my body, at its inability to move in harmony and in rhythm with the other body. Or is it a refusal? A resistance to being led by a man? I mean, I can and do dance and I love dancing. But not dancing like that, having to follow the man. Why can't he follow me?

We encountered forty-eight rebel checkpoints driving north through Ivory Coast. I relished having the opportunity to show J how good I was at negotiating with groups of young armed men. There was one particularly nerve-racking stop not far from Ferkessédougou. Seven or eight of them spread across the road. One had a rocket-propelled grenade resting on his shoulder. The others had an assortment of hunting rifles and Kalashnikovs and daggers tucked into their belts. We pulled up and they ordered us out of the car. I tried my usual offer of cigarettes. They weren't interested. They invited me, alone, to the shed. It looked like your average Chingford garden shed in blazing sun, set back nine metres from the road. Inside, a young man with an automatic rifle sat in a chair behind a desk. He was attractive and so friendly, it was disarming. We shared a bit of banter. I told him that we were driving to Mali, to live and work in Bamako. I probably slagged off the government in the south and the BBC in London before offering him cigarettes and a very small amount of money. I'm talking coins. The mood was jovial and increasingly less threatening. My memory of them is positive, possibly maternal.

Later, J and I argued about what had happened in the town of Bouake. We'd caught a glimpse of a large group of soldiers jogging in unison through town. The noise their feet made as they stamped down onto the tarmac was very intidimating. It was the perfect sound effect for a radio report, so I wanted to follow them to record it, but J had wanted to get going. I think he'd had enough of my obsession with all the men with their weapons.

There are things you learn in life which alter your perspective entirely. Like the fact that some people in the Midlands inject themselves with adrenaline and run as fast as they can through dense woods in the middle of the night without torches.

Smack into a tree, you can die.

That first week in Abidjan, the skies suddenly darkened when hundreds of fruit bats dropped from the branches of tall trees and began flapping in large circles outside the windows of the BBC offices on the fourth – or was it the fifth? – floor. Sirens interrupted their cackling and squawking and we spotted President Laurent Gbagbo's convoy oozing out of a side street on to the main road below. Like domesticated dogs fleeing a tsunami long before it hits, the swarming fruit bats were a warning.

One of my proudest moments was at a press conference in the Natural History Museum in Luanda. A senior US diplomat had been telling members of Angola's civil society what they could and should be doing to stop the war. He said that peace could only be won by Angolans. I can't remember his name now, but he had been a US secretary of state and his hair was white. It seemed to me outrageous hypocrisy, what he said. Why not start with an apology for what his country had done to foment the conflict? I was livid. I stood up and berated him and his government loud and clear. He replied with some sarcastic comment about the BBC's choice of reporter, implying that they must have made a mistake when hiring me. But a line of priests had already got to their feet and were clapping my words. Truly, this was a high point in my life.

To impress my brother and his friends, I drank malt vinegar from a bottle. I think they all clapped and my brother beamed with pride. I might be imagining that last bit, but it was certainly another high point.

On the underground the other day, I couldn't keep my eyes off this little girl. She must have been eight or nine years old and, I think, of Sri Lankan heritage. She was completely captivating. Yet, on her head, she wore the face of another little girl, the marshmallow cheeks and expanding blue eyes of a Disney princess whose fake yellow plaits lay on top of the real girl's shiny black hair, rudely framing her beautiful brown skin. Staring at the child, I thought of a friend, whose daughter hates her tight black curls and longs to be blonde like the other little girls at school.

When we were still at primary school, my sister and I nagged my mum to let us bicycle in on our own. Eventually, she gave in and, one day, off we went up Christchurch Road, passing The Plough, the wrought iron gates to the big house, and on towards the church. We knew there wasn't a bike shed at school, so we decided to leave them in some bushes on the common.

When we returned at the end of the day, our bikes had vanished. So we walked over towards the bowling green, to the park keeper's cottage. We banged on the door and a large man appeared in dungarees. We told him we wanted our bikes back and he started shouting, threatening us, telling us it was illegal to leave bikes on the common. My sister got upset. She began to cry. I became angry. I can't have been older than nine, and I didn't think twice about shouting back at the park keeper. I told him he had to give us back our bikes. Which, eventually, he did. Today, my sister thinks this was an early sign of my confrontational approach to life. She thinks it shows that I'm brave. But I don't feel brave: I feel angry.

Once, I found a lost little girl on Walthamstow market. She was standing, shouting through tears, at two men, who were looking at her with sideways glances. She spoke poor English. She couldn't remember where she lived, only the number on her front door. She kept saying a word like forest, so I guessed she lived on Forest Road. But when we arrived outside the house, she howled and shook her head furiously. In the end, after two hours wandering the streets, I took her to the police station because I didn't want to be accused of kidnapping. I returned home and searched the internet for streets sounding like forest in Walthamstow. I found one a few minutes away, and sped over on my bike. Sure enough, a frantic Polish family was having an upsetting argument.

I thought about buying that little Polish girl an *A to Z* of London, to help her explore her new neighbourhood more safely. But something stopped me returning to her house.

I remember, after Granny died, being shown Grandpa Robert's map. He'd made it by pouring candle wax onto a handkerchief when he was a prisoner of war in Neunkirchen in Germany during World War One. He managed to keep the map during two years of captivity and despite being searched several times by guards. My uncle still has that map. He says it depicts an area all the way to Holland, including various railways and transport routes.

I became pretty anxious the first time I found myself the other, the stranger, the only white person in a crowd of black faces. I was standing in a bus park on the outskirts of Accra. The fear came as a bit of a shock. I felt ashamed of myself. But that experience proved to be a revolutionary moment in my life. It unfurled a whole new way of thinking. I'd call it an epiphany.

During a sandstorm in southern Niger, I felt myself disappearing from the world. When eventually the wind dropped, I climbed back onto the little bus, the goats still strapped tight to the roof. We arrived in Niamey a few hours later. Today, whenever I think of that city, the same warming relief slips through me and I feel safe.

J says, You should have been a detective. Sometimes I say, I'm a modern Miss Marple. At other times I say, I'm a walking CCTV camera. But what self-respecting woman shares these thoughts with anyone, let alone publishes them in a book?

A few years ago – it was twenty past six in the morning – I was standing at my window, Salomão in my arms, gazing out on the street below, when two black saloon cars pulled up. Four men and a woman got out. One of the men stood at the boot of his car and began dressing up as a postman. He even had a Royal Mail bag. Then all five of them began walking towards the side of our house. I was still looking down at them when the woman looked up. She stopped. She said something to the men. They all looked up. I lifted a hand, a half-wave. They were obviously linked to the three burglars who'd tried to break into my neighbour's house. They'd come back. I ran out of my little office, into the bedroom, expecting to see them appear at the front of the house. But there was no one. They'd disappeared. I called J. Wake up! There's something very odd going on outside! He groaned under the duvet. I scanned the street and I noticed something moving behind the hedge in the front garden. I stood on my tiptoes. I could just see them, bending over, a line of five, on the other side of the privet. I pushed the window open and stuck my head out: What the fuck are you lot doing back here? Get the fuck out of here before I call the cops! At this, one of the men jumped out from behind the hedge and stood in front of our garden wall. He put his hand to his back pocket, pulled something from it, then swung his arm up in the air, pointing at me what I thought was going to be a gun but was just a small document. We're CID! We're doing a raid! Can you keep the noise down? At this, all five of them ran past our house, past the next one, and the next one, and then disappeared. A few minutes later another pair of saloon cars pulled up. Men wearing blue rubber gloves climbed out and stood preening themselves on the pavement. J shook his head. We had some tea. An hour later, a knock at the door. The pretend postman wanted to apologise. The large man at his side wanted to explain. That's the first time in twenty-one years I've been confronted by a member of the public on an early morning raid. It's reassuring, he said. Two days later, I chopped the hedge down to a stump.

I was in the front garden the following weekend. Three boys were playing football in the side street. That lady, I heard one of them shout, she's cut her head off! I peered around the corner, and they came running. Why did you cut it off? It had a nose and everything! I told them about the cops. I said I didn't want to have police, or anyone else, hiding behind my hedge. One of them piped up: My mum doesn't like the cops. She says they're racist. I told them about the time I'd shouted at a pair of police who were sitting on one of my neighbours, a young black man. The kid replied that this was the first day his mum had allowed him out in a month. Did you hear about the rape on Stoneydown? the kid asked. I nodded. I had. A terrible story. Well, my mum says I look a bit like one of the boys they're looking for. And he's got a flat-top. She's been afraid that I'd get nicked, but they arrested him yesterday so she says I can come out now. The kid looked at me seriously. Can you grow your hedge back? Will you make it back into a head? Give it a couple of years, I said, and the head will be here.

I've stopped shaving away the hair under my armpits, but I still shave my legs. I was upset when I heard a male friend describe women who shave as disgusting and childlike. Another male friend said he won't even talk to women who wear makeup. Last winter, I started wearing strong burgundy lipstick, the same colour as my favourite woolly hat. I bought the lipstick with a multi-lingual Portuguese friend who is also a novelist and an academic. I persuaded her to buy neoteny pink. What's wrong with that?

I dye my hair, but I specifically instruct my hairdresser not to dye the white bits. They're the bits I like. My first strands of white hair appeared within two weeks of returning from Malange. Sheer fear.

With my tights around my ankles, my jumper around my waist, I watched the doctor's finger follow my varicose veins. Earlier, he'd called the nurse in. I'd noticed the name on her badge. Omolara. She laughed when I told her my Omolara story. In Yoruba it means children are the heart of family, she said. I didn't want to tell her that I don't have any children. I was remembering a most unpleasant encounter in Luanda with the mother of a friend. She'd asked me how many children I had. When I said None, her head jerked back. You egoist!

Travelling in certain parts of west and southern Africa, I have on occasion lied and told people I have children. When they ask their names, I list my nephews and nieces.

The sound of a man beating his wife terrified me. A friend and I were staying with the couple in their house in Portugal. I had never actually heard domestic violence before. His occasional shouts; her absolute silence. My friend and I pushed a cupboard to our bedroom door then sat on the bed staring at each other but saying nothing. The following morning, I'd liked to have shot him. Instead, the four of us sat by the swimming pool drinking coffee and eating croissants.

By the time I was reporting in Ivory Coast in 2004, I had begun to question the relationship between the real and the imagination. And I began to engage more fully with the importance of doubt. This was the period when I started to think that perhaps the news world was not for me. It's the insistence on certainty that I most dislike.

I have listened to a science journalist talking about the ways that the brain always fills in for the eyes. When you see a cat sitting behind a lavender bush, for example, your brain fills in the bits of the cat that your eyes can't see. This helps you to understand what it is you are seeing. But what if the brain is wrong? What if the brain makes an assumption that is incorrect? An example of this might be the content of a message I received recently from a police constable. It read: I thought I'd found a hidden stash of drugs in the bushes just past your house, but unfortunately it turned out to be a bag full of very small snails.

I love the idea that I could be a Nigerian and that I have been a Nigerian, albeit in someone's head.

A long time ago, the owner of a sweet shop picked up my sister and put her inside a large freezer. Shopkeepers probably don't do that any more. Back then, though, we thought it was hilarious.

Thinking of that freezer reminds me of another one in a tower block in Luanda. A friend was cooking me a meal with meat he'd pulled from the freezer. As he smashed the thawing beef to pieces, the blood splattered, forming long red lines down the sides of the white cooling crate. I thought of this wonderful man before me, of how he had been tortured in the 1970s, and was made to suck his own blood off the floor of the prison.

Three years ago, I attended the funeral of an old friend who'd hanged himself. In the crematorium – everyone kept calling it "the crem" – I started thinking about the cat I'd seen hanging from its neck in Angola, and I felt bad about that. I felt bad, too, at the wake, while talking with one of my dead friend's friends, a striking woman with thick black wavy hair. It was close to dusk, and the last of the sun's rays were slipping from her locks, turning the outer curls a rich burgundy colour. She was telling me how confused she was and how much she was going to miss our friend. She had cried so much, her cheeks were stained with tears. Even so, I wasn't really listening because I was so enchanted by the light on her hair.

I regretted having short hair after a bus journey across north London. It was one of those old open-back double deckers that you could jump on and off between stops. The 38. Opposite me, a little boy was sat next to his mother, asking her over and over, Is that a man, mummy, or a woman? His mother said nothing. She tried to discourage him from speaking. She tried distracting him. But he wouldn't shut up. I don't know why it upset me so much. I think I was tiring of endlessly being mistaken for someone I wasn't. Either I was Jamie Lee Curtis, or I was a transvestite, or I was a boy. I couldn't bear it any more. I felt so paranoid after that journey, I stayed at home for several days, refusing to step outside the front door.

I became irritated with a friend of mine, an Angolan woman I hold dear. We were talking on Skype when she said, But you weren't really a proper war correspondent were you, Lara? I mean, you didn't hang out with the army all the time, did you? I became defensive and frustrated. We ended up sharing a long discussion about what it means to be a war correspondent and arguing about what war really means. In the end, she told me to Just cool it, Lara! and we both burst out laughing.

When I was still pregnant, the very gentle Egyptian doctor asked me, with no judgement whatsoever, Is this baby wanted? He then said, Books can always be written, but babies can't always be born.

Annie Zunz never had children. That was a Google search that surprised me.

I did go back. In 2002 and 2007 and 2008. I was searching for something. I think I wanted to get that feeling back, the feeling of belonging or having a role that actually matters. I also wanted to check up on my memory – a ridiculous plan, probably. I wanted to track down people who'd helped me. I wanted to say thank you to men like Sílvio, who drove me into a bombing zone so that I could witness, close up, what happens when a shell lands. We stood together, watching the bombs fall. Except they land at such a rate, you can't exactly see them: you experience them.

I found him having lunch in a café. I tapped him on the shoulder and he jumped in his chair. He remembered me instantly, but he said that my Portuguese was so vastly improved, it was hard to believe I was the same person. It was odd being able to communicate so much more easily than we ever had before. I had the chicken with me. I was carrying her in a plastic bag and had made a hole for her to poke her head through. I think Sílvio liked this. I told him that, in my hotel room, I was keeping her tied to the shower taps. If you don't believe me, this is one of the few things I photographed.

I wanted to find the truck driver, too. I wanted to thank him. And I wanted to meet his daughter, Lara. *Minha xará*. My namesake. And it was Sílvio who helped me.

On my very last morning in Malange, we tracked down the truck driver's house on the outskirts of town. As we approached, two women stepped outside and cried out, It's Lara! I had never met them before, yet they knew who I was. The truck driver's aunt and his sister. But he was not there. Shortly after the war ended, he was killed in a car crash on the same road that he had travelled month after month, year after year, avoiding ambushes and landmines. As an offering, I gave the women my chicken. I worried this was a betrayal to the king, but I was also attracted to the idea of the continuation of the gift.

A couple of days later, trudging for hours around the shantytowns of Luanda, asking people for the lady from Malange who sells alcohol, I found little Lara. She told me that when she grows up she wants to be a journalist. We took some photographs and her younger brother led me to the picture developers so that we could share them out that very day. I remember a woman shouting at me as I walked through the lanes with the boy, his hand cupped in mine. You should buy him some shoes! Shame on you! She spat at the ground.

For a long time, I kept a photograph of Lara pinned to the board above my desk. She is standing beside me, I have my arm around her waist. I am smiling, she is concentrating on the camera. Now, that photo lies in a drawer among piles of images of my nephews and nieces and others in my life. You know, I've never done anything for that little girl. Nothing at all.

The roses were a gift from my mother-in-law. They're climbing furiously up the house, trying to claw their way inside. They'll be at the bedroom window by the end of summer. It's hard tying knots when you're wearing suede gloves. I think of Salomão, at half-past-five in the morning, tending to his garden and the many potted plants that have surrounded his Luanda home for ninety years. A light tap on the shutters and his wrinkled fingers would appear, offering me *maracuja* plucked fresh from the tree. That's Portuguese for passion fruit.

In 2011, fifty-seven-year-old Philmore Mills was admitted to Wexham Park hospital in Slough with pneumonia. He had a tumour on his right lung. I read about him because of something someone had tweeted. He was placed face down on the floor, his hands cuffed behind his back and his legs restrained by police. He was sweating and struggling to breathe, according to the nurse in charge on the night he died. I noticed the tweet because of the words Wexham Park. That's where I was with my fractured pelvis.

Hilário and I met on a boat on the Thames over a decade ago. He was with a friend who was dressed as a standard lamp with a large shade over her head. People were kissing strangers through a hole in a sheet. A Portuguese man wearing dark glasses was speaking Russian to no one in particular. And a woman with lots of hair was playing uncanny chords on a cello. That night, Hilário wasn't the only Angolan on the boat. My friend Zé was there too. They hadn't laid eyes on each other in nearly thirty years. You should have heard the laughter.

The other day, over a coffee on the market, Hilário looked at me with rare seriousness. Why haven't you gone back? he asked. Tell me the truth, Lara. I felt myself wince. Money, I said. Desire, I said. Fear, I said. But I've been thinking about his question ever since.

And I've been thinking about the nuns, about the walk I took with Sister around the Hanga Mission in Bailundo. She led me down an avenue of eucalyptus trees, peeling bark revealing silver. The aroma swept me to my grandfather's house, a bachelor's pad of walls stained nicotine-yellow in Weybridge, to Walter Wanderley's organ and my mother's demands to Dance! Come on, kids! and to shake that fish feeder full of raw rice. On the other side of my grandfather's garden wall, where the Siamese cat became a sculpture in stone, the grounds of an old people's home full of eucalyptus and vast, elegant pines, where we played with our cousins for hours while the grown-ups snoozed after lunch.

Sister pointed into the distance, to an amphitheatre, where smoke was twisting from the stage floor, around the columns, to the arches of the ceiling above. I could see flames and slight movement and as we stepped closer, I heard a mumbling interrupted by laughter. Closer still, the outline of a man stepping through the smoke, a red scarf tied tight around his head and knotted, pirate-like, at the back. Come, look! said Sister. I walked forward to what I had assumed was the edge of the seating area but was, instead, a swimming pool, drained of water, dust and leaves banked up in the corners, and the steps rusting at either end. Several little boys were running around inside, kicking a tennis ball, shouting and laughing. Sister beckoned me alongside her and as we walked towards the stage, it began to transform. I could see a crucifix high up on the back wall. Beneath it, a woman working a fire to heat a casserole pot hanging over the flames. They've been living here since the war, said Sister. They won't go home. She called out a greeting to anyone who was listening. *Walale pó?* A few hands lifted and I heard an echo of voices.

This is where the altar was, explained Sister, lifting a finger at the stage. The congregation would have sat there, where the swimming pool is, because it was a church, you see. But the old man, who was murdered, pulled it down and he built another church over there. She indicated a large rectangular building some way off to the right and I thought how tired she looked. She wore the expression of someone who has seen it all a thousand times. I followed her past the altar, down the narrow path to the left. She ran a finger along the cracks in the stone work. It could all fall down, she said. We walked past the classrooms where the old man used to teach the novices. Some of the windows were missing, blown out by bombs and bangs and bullets many moons ago. Everywhere, chopped wood was stacked up. A radio was playing. Two avocado trees were dripping in fruit, fat and full. A narrow path twisted in the grass and we came out beside a row of outhouses, low buildings where pigs might once have been kept or cattle or feed or perhaps a small tractor. At the far end, a narrow door no higher than my chest. Sister slammed her knuckles into the heavy wood: *Walale pó?* The door juddered. A hand was gripping to one side, pulling it inwards. The face of an old man moved into the light. He wore a waistcoat over his yellow shirt. His trousers were tied with string. His feet were bare and his toenails so rotten they made my obsession with my own fungal toenail quite pathetic.

We have a guest, said Sister.

From where? replied the old man.

Ami tchingelesi, I said, proud to practise my rudimentary Umbundu.

Oh, England, England! That's a long way away, England! He laughed and I got a brief glimpse of his pink tongue. He turned his back to us and retreated a couple of steps inside. I could hear him talking to another, to someone out of view. A shuffling sound and an old woman appeared at his side. She wore a crimson wrap. She raised her hand, her breast stretching up with her arm. She exchanged greetings with Sister in Umbundu and Portuguese. The old man switched his gaze away from the nun, muttering words I did not understand. He reached towards my hand, curling his fingers into my palm, his hand as cold as water.

I was born in 1933, he said. I have never left my land, despite the war, despite everything.

Sister picked up. In 1999, he had to flee his village and he came here, to this building, and here he has remained ever since.

The old man looked to me then back to her. When is she leaving? he asked.

Probably tomorrow, said the nun.

He waved a hand. Oh she can't do that. She must stay longer.

Sister explained my plans to travel to Cabinda, far away to the north, but the old man shook his head. Don't do that, he said. Stay here. This is Angola. It is here. This is the place to be.